# THE U.S. ARMY IN

# WORLD WAR II

*A Pictorial Record*

# THE U.S. ARMY IN
# WORLD WAR II

## A Pictorial Record

VOLUME I

## THE WAR AGAINST GERMANY:

*Europe and Adjacent Areas*

■

*Compiled by the Center of*
*Military History United States Army*

ARTABRAS · PUBLISHERS · NEW YORK

The U.S. Army in World War II: A Pictorial Record

VOLUME I
The War Against Germany:
Europe and Adjacent Areas

VOLUME II
The War Against Germany and Italy:
The Mediterranean and Adjacent Areas

VOLUME III
The War Against Japan

Library of Congress Cataloging-in-Publication Data

The War against Germany.

Reprint. Originally published: Washington, D.C.: Office of the Chief of
Military History, Dept. of the Army, 1951. (United States Army in
World War II. Pictorial record)
1. World War, 1939–1945—Campaigns—Western—Pictorial
works.   I. Series: United States Army in World War II.
Pictorial record.
D756.W35 1990                     940.54'21                     90-604
ISBN 0-89660-010-6

. . . to Those Who Served

# UNITED STATES ARMY IN WORLD WAR II

Kent Roberts Greenfield, General Editor

## *Advisory Committee*

## *Office of the Chief of Military History*

Maj. Gen. Orlando Ward, Chief

# Foreword

During World War II the photographers of the United States armed forces created on film a pictorial record of immeasurable value. Thousands of pictures are preserved in the photographic libraries of the armed services but are little seen by the public.

In the narrative volumes of UNITED STATES ARMY IN WORLD WAR II, now being prepared by the Office of the Chief of Military History of the United States Army, it is possible to include only a limited number of pictures. Therefore, a subseries of pictorial volumes, of which this is one, has been planned to supplement the other volumes of the series. The photographs have been especially selected to show important terrain features, types of equipment and weapons, living and weather conditions, military operations, and matters of human interest. These volumes will preserve and make accessible for future reference some of the best pictures of World War II. An appreciation not only of the terrain upon which actions were fought, but also of its influence on the capabilities and limitations of weapons in the hands of both our troops and those of the enemy, can be gained through a careful study of the pictures herein presented. These factors are essential to a clear understanding of military history.

This book deals with the European Theater of Operations, covering the period from the build-up in the United Kingdom through V-E Day. Its seven sections are arranged chronologically. The photographs were selected and the text written by Capt. Kenneth E. Hunter; the editing was done by Miss Mary Ann Bacon. The written text has been kept to a minimum. The appendixes give information as to the abbreviations used and the sources of the photographs.

ORLANDO WARD
Maj. Gen., USA
Chief of Military History

Washington, D. C.
6 February 1951

# Contents

# THE BUILD-UP
# IN THE UNITED KINGDOM
# AND THE
# AIR OFFENSIVE, EUROPE

# The Build-up in the United Kingdom and the Air Offensive, Europe*

The build-up of the United States Army in the United Kingdom, from January 1942 until June 1944, with the huge amounts of supplies necessary to equip and maintain the forces and to prepare for the invasion of northern Europe was a tremendous undertaking. It involved the transportation of men and supplies across the Atlantic during a time when the German submarine menace was at its peak. The United States Navy played a vital role in transporting men and supplies and in protecting the convoys while en route. During this period the administrative task was enormous since facilities for quartering and training such large forces and for storing supplies and equipment had to be provided within the limited area of the United Kingdom. In October 1942 some of the units stationed in the United Kingdom were sent to the Mediterranean for the invasion of North Africa. The build-up continued after this, well-trained units arriving from the United States. As the time for the invasion of France approached, battle-tested units from the Mediterranean theater were transferred to England to prepare for their part in the assault. In spite of the limited terrain available, large-scale maneuvers and realistic amphibious operations were conducted. In the early spring of 1944 joint exercises of the ground, sea, and air forces which were to make the attack in Normandy were held along the southern coast of England. The last of these exercises was held in early May, the units then moving to the staging areas and embarkation points for the invasion.

While the ground forces were being equipped and trained the Allied air forces bombed the fortress of Europe. The Royal Air Force

*See Gordon A. Harrison, *Cross-Channel Attack,* Washington, D. C., 1951.

Bomber Command carried out the air assault by night and the United States Eighth Air Force by day. The first U.S. participation in the bombing of Europe from British bases was on 4 July 1942, when American crews flew six British bombers. During the fall of 1942 the Eighth Air Force prepared the Twelfth Air Force for the invasion of Africa, and it was not until the beginning of 1943 that U.S. bombers began to attack Europe from England in large-scale raids. From that time on the attacks on Germany continued with increasing intensity and shattering power until, in February 1944, the German Luftwaffe attempted to sweep the U. S. bombers from the skies over Europe. After a battle of one week's duration over important industrial cities of Germany, the Luftwaffe was beaten and supremacy of the air was in Allied hands where it remained until the end of the war.

U. S. TROOPS arriving in Belfast, Northern Ireland. The first U. S. troops to cross the Atlantic after the declaration of war by the United States went to Northern Ireland in January 1942. In the same month the Special Observer Group was replaced by Headquarters, United States Armed Forces in the British Isles. Shortly thereafter the center of concentration was transferred from Ireland to England and the rapid build-up of personnel commenced. Logistical planning began in April 1942. This build-up of men and supplies was to become one of the greatest logistical undertakings in military history. Supplies were shipped from the United States in ever increasing quantities until, during the month of June 1944, approximately 1,000,000 long tons were received in the United Kingdom.

U. S. TROOPS marching through the streets of a town in Northern Ireland escorted by a British sergeant. The first U. S. troops to arrive in Ireland were 18 officers and 18 enlisted men, the advance party for the first contingent. By 1 June 1944 there were 1,562,000 U. S. troops in the United Kingdom. During the early months after the United States' entry into World War II a large part of the equipment was similar to that of World War I. In the succeeding months much was done to improve all types of equipment and many of the changes may be seen in the pictures that follow in this volume.

TRAINING IN IRELAND, FEBRUARY 1942. Before leaving the United States members of the U. S. armed forces normally had completed their training, but to keep the men at the peak of their fighting fitness programs in firing, field exercises, and special problems were begun under varying weather and terrain conditions. Men in their late teens or early twenties made the finest soldiers as they had stamina and recuperative power far beyond that of older men. This physical superiority often determined the issue in heavy and prolonged fighting.

INFANTRYMAN WITH WEAPONS. Soldier is holding a .45-caliber Thompson submachine gun M1928A1; from left to right are: 60-mm. mortar M2, British anti-tank gun, .30-caliber U. S. rifle M1 with bayonet M1 attached, .30-caliber Browning machine gun M1919A4, hand grenades, .45-caliber automatic pistol M1911A1, .30-caliber U. S. rifle M1903 with grenade launcher M1 attached, .30-caliber Browning automatic rifle M1913A2, and 81-mm. mortar M1 (top). Infantryman has just completed an obstacle course (bottom).

SOLDIERS LAND FROM AN ASSAULT BOAT during a training exercise in Scotland, July 1942. The base of fire of a rifle platoon was its automatic weapons. The riflemen concentrated their fire on the impact area blocked out by the automatic weapons. The base of fire of a U. S. rifle squad in World War II was the Browning automatic rifle (BAR). The man in right foreground is armed with this weapon. The two men behind the soldier with the BAR are armed with .30-caliber U. S. rifles M1.

TWO TYPES OF U. S. HEAVY, FOUR-ENGINED BOMBERS. Consolidated B–24 Liberators on a bombing mission over Europe (top); Boeing B–17 Flying Fortresses dropping bombs on enemy installations in Bremen, Germany, while flak bursts around them (bottom). The first U. S. air unit to engage in combat over Europe was a light bombardment squadron. Flying British planes, six U. S. crews joined six RAF crews in a daylight attack against four airdromes in the Netherlands on 4 July 1942. On 17 August twelve B–17's, accompanied by four RAF Spitfire fighter squadrons, attacked the marshalling yards at Rouen, France, and successfully completed the first U. S. attack over Europe. From these small beginnings the number of planes taking part in the raids grew until the average per raid in 1943 was 570 heavy bombers, a figure that was to be almost doubled in 1944.

THREE TYPES OF ESCORT FIGHTER PLANES over England. From top to bottom: Lockheed P–38 Lightning, North American P–51 Mustang, Republic P–47 Thunderbolt. P–47's were the first to join the British Spitfires in providing escort for heavy bombers, the P–38 was available in small numbers in October 1943, and the P–51 began to appear in January 1944. At first the 47's flew top cover, but before long they began to drop down and engage the enemy fighter planes. As the war progressed the escort opened out more and more until it became a huge net to envelop the enemy.

A BRITISH POLICE SERGEANT gives road direction to a U. S. first sergeant during a march. By the end of June 1944 there was a total of 140,656 Negro personnel in the European Theater of Operations assigned to both combat and service units. The M1 helmet worn by the sergeant was standardized on 9 June 1941, and mass production began shortly thereafter. It replaced the earlier M1917A1 helmet shown in preceding pictures.

MEMBERS OF THE FIRST OFFICER CANDIDATE SCHOOL (OCS) in the
United Kingdom decontaminating a building that has been subjected to mustard gas
(top). Machine gun training at OCS (bottom). Qualified enlisted men were selected
from units stationed in the British Isles and sent to this school where, upon the successful completion of the courses of instruction, they were commissioned second lieuten-
ants in the Army of the United States. The first class began in September 1942 and
there were in all seven classes, each lasting for approximately three months. The
OCS in England graduated and commissioned a total of 472 men.

A FIGHTER PILOT, standing beside his plane in England, wearing an oxygen mask and helmet equipped with earphones. Over his leather flying jacket is a life preserver. A number of young men from the United States joined the Canadian and British air forces before America's entry in the war. When the U. S. declared war these pilots were transferred to the U. S. air force. The strength of the U. S. air force in 1940 was about 43,000 men and 2,500 planes. In early 1944 there were 2,300,000 men and 80,000 aircraft.

INTERIOR OF A B–17 showing two .50-caliber Browning machine guns. These planes were highly complex machines, well armed, with machine guns in front, rear, sides, top, and bottom. The man in the picture is working on the gun turret which protruded beneath the fuselage. The tank on top of this turret was for oxygen.

AN ORDNANCE SPECIALIST in the repair of optical equipment cleans a pair
of field glasses, England, September 1942. Ordnance responsibility extended to
"everything that rolls, shoots, is shot, or is dropped from the air." Its complete cata-
logue contained 35,000 separate items, ranging from watch springs and firing pins
to 20-ton howitzers and 40-ton tanks.

A REPAIRED M3 MEDIUM TANK is given final check by Ordnance personnel. Every tank, gun, or vehicle, damaged either by an accident or later in combat, which could be repaired meant one less new tank to be supplied. As the war progressed the medium tank underwent changes as did a great deal of other U. S. equipment. It became lower so as to present a more difficult target, the riveted hull was replaced by a welded or cast hull, and toward the end of the war the suspension system was changed. These, and other mechanical changes, with the addition of better armament and armor, made the vehicle a more formidable fighting machine, better able to combat enemy tanks.

PARATROOPERS having their parachutes inspected before taking off for a practice jump, England, October 1942. These troops were equipped with specially designed clothing and equipment including helmets with a new type fiber liner and chin strap, jump suits with large pockets that could be securely fastened, and boots that laced higher up the leg and which had reinforced toes and stronger ankle supports.

SOLDIER BEING TRAINED in the correct method of attack when armed with
a knife. Note the difference between the uniform worn by the infantryman here
and that worn by paratroopers on opposite page.

AN ENGINEER COMPANY AT WORK ON AN AIRFIELD in England. By
1 June 1944 a total of 129 airfields was available in the United Kingdom for the
Eighth and Ninth Air Forces. In addition there were 3 base air depots, 7 combat
crew and replacement centers, 2 reconnaissance and 1 photographic reconnaissance
fields, 19 troop carrier fields, 11 advance landing grounds, and 2 miscellaneous fields.
Living quarters for more than 400,000 air force personnel had to be furnished, plus
many thousands of square feet of space for storage.

B–17 LANDING, after having dropped two flares to indicate that it has wounded crew members aboard, while two medical crews stand by to give first aid to the wounded (top). During raids over enemy territory crew members were sometimes wounded by flak or gunfire from enemy fighter planes. A crew member receiving medical attention as soon as his plane lands (bottom). In this case blood plasma is being administered. Blood plasma, which is whole blood minus the corpuscles, was given to those who had lost blood or were in shock. The plasma increased the volume of blood and kept the blood stream going. When casualties arrived at a hospital whole blood was administered to replace the blood lost and also to relieve shock before further treatment was begun.

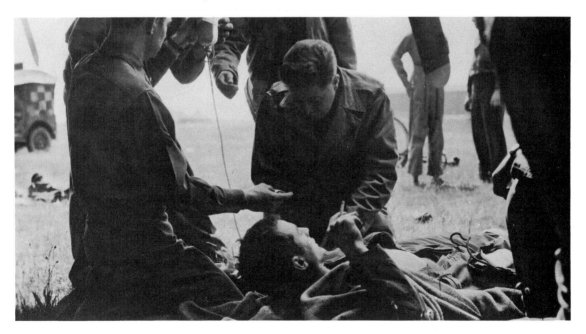

ENLISTED MEN OF THE ORDNANCE DEPARTMENT operating caterpillar tractor cranes to unload a crated gun carriage (half-track) which weighed approximately 20,000 pounds. The Ordnance Department maintained a large depot at Tidworth, England.

BOMBS BEING UNLOADED at a U. S. Air Corps Ordnance Depot in England. After being stacked the bombs were covered with camouflage nets such as those behind tractors at left center of picture. Facilities for storing bombs in any other manner were limited. These stacks became common sights along the country lanes and roads in England during the war years. (1,000-pound bombs; crawler-type revolving crane on tractor mounting with diesel engine.)

MEDIUM M3 TANKS in an Ordnance Depot, England (top). Combat tracked vehicles temporarily stored before being issued to the using units (bottom). After a vehicle arrived in the United Kingdom there was much to be done before it could be issued to the using unit. Tanks were received from the United States with about 500 items of accessory equipment, including small arms, radio, tools, gun sights, and other incidentals, packed in waterproofed containers; many were coated with a rust-preventive compound. The job of preparing an M4 tank took approximately fifty working hours. Accessories were unpacked, cleaned, tested, and installed; the motor and all mechanical components were checked and tuned. When a vehicle left the Ordnance depot it was completely supplied, including ammunition and rations.

A 105-MM. HOWITZER MOTOR CARRIAGE M7 on maneuvers in England, March 1943. This was an open-top, lightly armored vehicle and was the principal artillery weapon of an armored division.

U. S. NAVY PLANE attacks and sinks a German submarine in the North Atlantic, June 1943. The sinking of a British liner without warning by a German submarine off the coast of Scotland on 3 September 1939 opened the battle of the Atlantic, which continued until 14 May 1945 when the last U-boats surrendered at American Atlantic ports. Enemy submarines, traveling alone or in wolf packs, sank many Allied ships but by the middle of 1943 the menace had been reduced to a problem. This was accomplished by the use of the interlocking convoy system that provided escort protection along the important convoy routes, small escort aircraft carriers and destroyer escorts, and planes, from which hunter-killer groups were formed to seek out and destroy the U-boats.

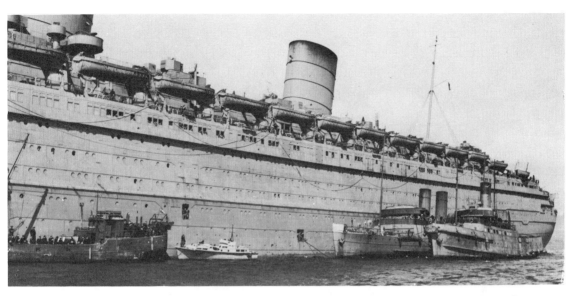

LIGHTERS PULL ALONGSIDE THE *QUEEN ELIZABETH* to unload U. S. troops in Scotland (top). Representatives of the American Red Cross serving refreshments to Waacs who have just arrived in Scotland (bottom). On one trip the *Queen Elizabeth* carried a record load of 15,028 troops. Between December 1941 and June 1944 the *Queen Mary* and the *Queen Elizabeth* transported a large portion of the total number of troops to the United Kingdom, running alone through seas in which their great speed was their chief protection against enemy submarines.

BOMBS TUMBLE FROM THE BAYS OF AN OVERTURNED B–24 BOMBER.
The plane was caught in a heavy flak belt while on a mission over Germany. During
1943 the enemy became much more aggressive as he shifted his fighters from the
Russian front and the Mediterranean theater to western Europe. The German day
fighters continually harassed U. S. heavy bombers, sometimes following them far out
to sea on their withdrawal.

A ROYAL AIR FORCE SEA RESCUE LAUNCH picking up the crew of a B–17 which crashed into the North Sea while returning to its base in England after a bombing raid over Germany. The crew members are in rubber boats and are flying a kite to which is attached the aerial of a short wave radio used to signal and give their position to the rescue craft. Many bombers were shot down over enemy territory and their crews captured, killed, or wounded; others were badly damaged and crashed into the North Sea on their return; while still others managed to return to their bases even though damaged. Many crews of the planes forced down at sea were rescued in the manner shown here.

SOLDIERS PLACING A BANGALORE TORPEDO under barbed wire during a training problem in England, August 1943. When fired, the charge would explode and clear a path through the obstruction. This method was not only faster than cutting through the wire, but also did not expose the men unnecessarily to enemy fire.

MEMBERS OF AN AIRBORNE DIVISION loading a ¼-ton 4x4 truck into a British Horsa glider (top). By removing the tail section, the glider could be unloaded in approximately seven minutes. Airborne infantrymen in a U. S. glider (bottom). In this picture men are armed with .30-caliber U. S. rifles M1903A3; .30-caliber U. S. rifles M1; .45-caliber Thompson submachine gun M1; 2.36-inch rocket launcher M1A1; and .30-caliber Browning automatic rifle M1918A2. Machine guns, mortars, and light artillery weapons were dropped by parachutes and brought in by gliders along with other supplies which made the airborne troops a compact fighting unit.

AERIAL VIEW OF SCHWEINFURT, GERMANY, October 1943. This city was the center of the ball-bearing factories, one of the target priorities picked for destruction by the strategic air force. The order of these priorities was as follows: (1) submarine construction yards and bases, (2) aircraft industry, (3) ball-bearing industry, (4) oil industry, (5) synthetic rubber plants, and (6) military transport vehicle industry. The Schweinfurt raid had considerable significance at this time because the Americans were still trying to prove the feasibility of daylight precision bombing. This crucial raid was made by a force of 228 heavy bombers and there ensued one of the greatest battles in Eighth Air Force history. From the German frontier at Aachen, where the fighter escort had to leave the bombers because of limited gasoline capacities, to Schweinfurt and return wave after wave of enemy fighters attacked the bombers.

**BOMBS STRIKING THE BALL-BEARING FACTORIES** at Schweinfurt, Germany, October 1943. Flak over the target was intense but good visibility enabled the bombers to make an accurate run and more than 450 tons of high explosives and incendiaries were dropped in the target area. Heavy damage was inflicted on the major plants. The cost to the attackers was also severe. Sixty-two bombers were lost and 138 were damaged. Personnel casualties were 599 killed and 40 wounded. Such losses could not be sustained and deep penetrations without escort were suspended. Schweinfurt was not attacked again for four months and the Germans were given a chance to take countermeasures, which they did with great energy and skill.

HEAVY BOMBERS ON A MISSION over southwestern Germany, December 1943. Planes at upper level are Boeing B–17's; those at lower level are Consolidated B–24's. After the Schweinfurt raid unescorted bomber raids were discontinued until 1944 when long-range fighters equipped with wing tanks were able to provide fighter escort for the B–17's and B–24's as far as Berlin. By 1944 the Luftwaffe, although still offering a formidable defense, basically had decayed and was very vulnerable to Allied air power that was being concentrated against it. By April 1944 the Allies had achieved air superiority which permitted full-scale air attacks on Germany, an indispensable prerequisite for the invasion of Normandy.

B–17's DROPPING BOMBS OVER BREMEN, December 1943. Control of the air started with an attack on the Focke-Wulf plant at Bremen in April 1943, but the main attacks did not get under way until that summer. On six successive days in late July Allied air forces attacked the German aircraft industry so successfully that the production rate started downward. It was not until February 1944 that the decisive air battle came, when for a period of six days of perfect weather a continuous assault on the widely dispersed German aircraft-frame factories and assembly plants seriously reduced the capabilities of the Luftwaffe. Subsequent attacks affected the entire aircraft industry and it never fully recovered.

BRITISH FIRE FIGHTERS combating a fire started by bombs during a German
night attack over London, February 1944. The Battle of Britain began in August
1940 and continued on a large scale through October. During the air blitz over
England the Luftwaffe suffered irreparable losses from which its bombardment arm
never recovered, even though smaller attacks were carried out until late in the war.
In daytime raids over England during the Battle of Britain from August to October
1940, the Germans lost 2,375 planes and crews, while the British lost 375 pilots.

A BRITISH SPITFIRE FIGHTER chasing a German V-bomb over England. Only fast low-level ships, such as the British Spitfire or the U. S. P–47 or P–51, were good at this type of pursuit since the robot bombs averaged well over 300 miles per hour. These bombs, launched from sites along the invasion coast of France and the Low Countries, caused considerable damage in England and in addition were a demoralizing factor in that one never knew when or where they would strike. The launching sites were placed on the list of targets for the Allied air forces, but because these sites could be easily moved and camouflaged they were not completely destroyed until the invasion forces took over the areas in which they were located. The first of the V-bombs appeared over England on 13 June 1944.

MEMBERS OF AN ENGINEER UNIT operating multiplex machines in the process of preparing maps from aerial mosaics. Relief and other features were plotted from photographic diapositives, contained in the conical shaped holders on the beam in background of lower picture, to sheets on which control and check points have been plotted. In these two photographs contours are being drawn on the maps by use of the multiplex machine. Contrary to general opinion, France was not a well-mapped country. During World War I detailed maps showed primarily trench fortifications and special small areas. The Engineers were responsible for making maps, which required the services of highly trained personnel.

MEMBERS OF AN ENGINEER TOPOGRAPHICAL BATTALION preparing maps of Europe prior to the invasion of France. In 1944 more than 125,000,000 maps giving more complete details than those shown here were printed for the invasion alone. An average of 867 tons of maps was shipped each month from the United States. In addition, 3,695,750 salvaged enemy maps were used for reverse side printing. Large-scale maps showing beach and underwater obstacles on the American and British assault beaches were produced by the U. S. Army Engineers in preparation for the invasion.

ANEMOMETER AND WIND DIRECTION INDICATOR being checked by an enlisted man of a weather section. Improvements in weather forecasting, instrument bombing technique and equipment, and operating procedures had advanced so much that whereas in 1942 U. S. bombers could operate on an average of only six days per month, in the last year of the war they averaged twenty-two days.

MEMBERS OF A FIGHTER GROUP being briefed before taking off on a mission, England, 1944.

WACS WORKING IN THE COMMUNICATIONS SECTION of the operations room at an air force station. No opportunity was overlooked to replace men with personnel of the Women's Army Corps both in the United States and overseas. Wacs were given many technical and specialized jobs to do, as well as administrative and office work. The Medical Corps employed the largest number of Wacs in technical jobs, but other technical services such as the Transportation Corps, Signal Corps, Ordnance Department, and Quartermaster Corps had many positions that could be performed by women as efficiently as by men.

MAIL FOR UNITS STATIONED IN ENGLAND being sorted. The handling of the mails through the Army Post Office (APO) was a function of the Adjutant General's Department. Mail normally was delivered to the armed forces with the least possible delay as it was an important morale factor for men stationed away from home. During the last week of May 1944 an artificial delay of ten days was imposed on the forwarding of all American mail to the United States and elsewhere, and the use of transatlantic telephone, radio, and cable facilities was denied to American personnel. British mail was strictly censored by the military authorities from April 1944 until the invasion on 6 June 1944. These precautionary measures were taken to assure the secrecy of the coming invasion. In addition, a block was also placed on diplomatic correspondence of all countries except the United States, Great Britain, and the USSR.

ARTILLERY UNITS TRAINING IN ENGLAND. A liaison plane flying over a battery of 105-mm. howitzers M2A1 (top). A 155-mm. gun firing (bottom).

155-MM. GUNS AND 105-MM. HOWITZERS (top and bottom respectively) stored in England, 1944. After about 2,250 rounds had been fired, the barrel of the 155-mm. gun had to be replaced; in howitzers the number of rounds was higher.

DIESEL LOCOMOTIVES, TANK CARS, AND FREIGHT CARS lined up in England to be used on the Continent after the invasion (top). Caterpillar tractors and bulldozers stored at an Engineer depot to be used after the invasion of France (bottom).

20 GROSVENOR SQUARE, LONDON, U. S. Headquarters of the European Theater of Operations (top). U. S. enlisted men passing Number 10, Downing Street, residence and office of the Prime Minister of Great Britain (bottom). During the period of the build-up in the British Isles, activities and plans were formulated for the large and small units scattered throughout the United Kingdom in a group of buildings located near the American embassy in London. This group of buildings housed the offices of the personnel whose task it was to co-ordinate the activity and training of units and, in addition, to handle the problems relating to the build-up of supplies for the invasion.

A COLUMN OF HALF-TRACKS advancing along a road during the training period in England (top). The second, third, and fourth vehicles in the picture are 75-mm. gun motor carriages M3. This was the first standardized U. S. self-propelled antitank weapon used in World War II, and provided high mobility for the 75-mm. gun. It was replaced in March 1944 by the 76-mm. motor gun carriage M18, and in September 1944 was declared obsolete. Temporarily stored half-tracks (bottom). These vehicles were used as gun and howitzer motor carriages, antiaircraft gun carriages, and personnel carriers

ARMORED UNITS PARTICIPATING IN MANEUVERS in England. In the spring of 1944 intensified training was given to all units which were to take part in the invasion of Normandy. Light tank M5A1 (top), medium tank M4A1 (bottom). The U. S. tank was designed as a weapon of exploitation to be used in long-range thrusts deep into the enemy's rear where it could attack his supply installations and communications. This required great endurance, low consumption of gasoline, and ability to move long distances without a break-down.

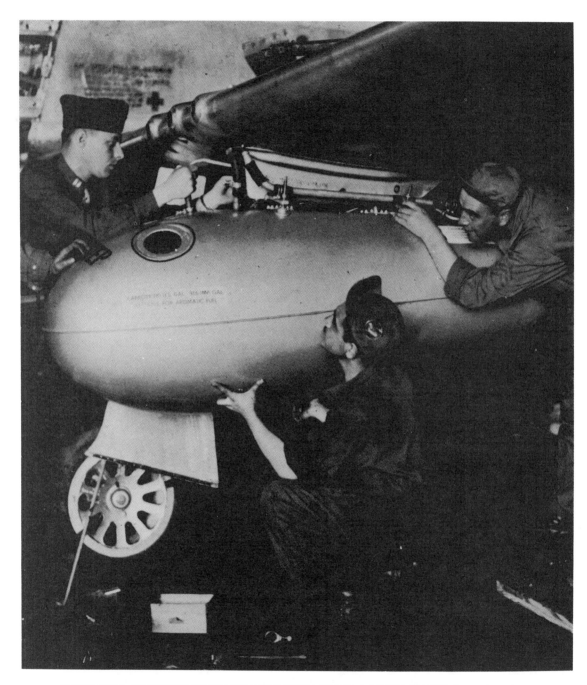

MEN OF A SERVICE SQUADRON SALVAGING A FUEL TANK from the wing
of a P–51. These tanks helped to make the bomber escort planes into long-range planes
which gave fighter protection to the heavy bombers. The tanks, the fuel from which
was consumed first, were dropped when empty and the plane then used gasoline from
its permanent tanks.

P–51'S IN FORMATION. Each plane in this formation has two wing tanks attached.

A MEDICAL BATTALION QUARTERED IN TENTS, Cornwall, England (top).
A U. S. hospital installed in Quonset huts (bottom). The hospital plan in the United
Kingdom called for over 90,000 beds in existing installations, conversions, and new
constructions. The program was later increased by 30,000 beds by using tents for the
hospital units.

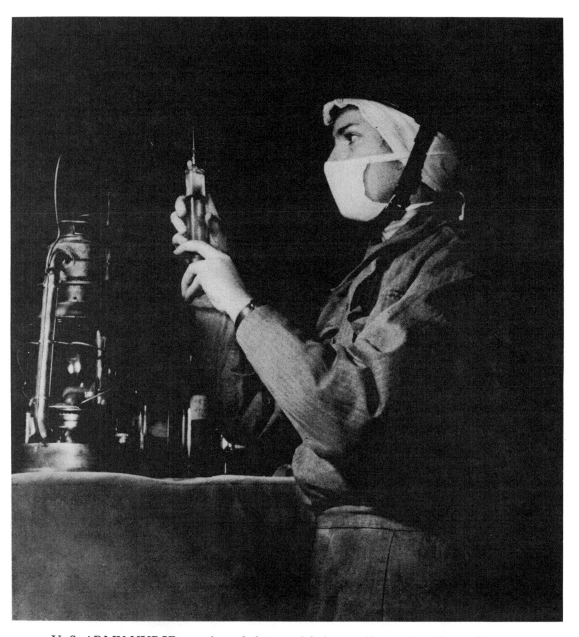

U. S. ARMY NURSE, wearing a helmet and fatigue uniform, preparing an intravenous injection; a kerosene lamp provides illumination. Hospital personnel worked under conditions similar to those they might encounter upon their arrival on the Continent after the invasion. Army nurses gave widely varying types of skilled service, some of them in field hospitals and others in the general hospitals farther behind the lines. World War II was the first war in which nurses received full military benefits and real instead of relative officer rank. There were more than 17,000 Army nurses in the ETO in May 1945.

FIRING GERMAN WEAPONS. In order to become familiar with German weapons and to learn the capabilities of enemy arms, U. S. infantrymen fired them during training in Northern Ireland in the spring of 1944. The men in the top picture are firing a German standard dual-purpose machine gun (7.92-mm. *M. G. 34*). The soldier in the bottom picture is firing a German rifle (7.92-mm. *Karbiner 98K–Mauser-Kar. 98K*) which was the standard shoulder weapon of the German Army and very similar to the U. S. rifle M1903.

MEMBERS OF AN ARMORED INFANTRY REGIMENT firing U. S. weapons during training in England. In 1941 the Ordnance Department began its experiments with the rocket launcher, which resulted in the invention of the 2.36-inch rocket launcher (bazooka). This was the first weapon of its type to be used in the war. Designed originally as an antitank weapon, it was used effectively against machine gun nests, pillboxes, and even fortified houses. It required only a two-man team—a gunner and a loader—and as it weighed only a little more than a rifle it could be carried everywhere (top). The crew of a 60-mm. mortar M2 firing at a simulated enemy position (bottom).

AN ENLISTED MAN ON GUARD DUTY at a rail junction in Wales where American-made locomotives were stored. The United States shipped 1,000 locomotives and 20,000 railroad cars to the United Kingdom for use on the Continent after the invasion. In addition, 270 miles of railroad were constructed in England to facilitate movements. The Transportation Corps was responsible for the movement of men and supplies by land and water, and for the operation and supply of a great deal of this equipment. Since much of the railroad equipment in Europe had been destroyed or damaged by preinvasion bombing by the Allied air forces, locomotives and cars had to be supplied by both the United States and the United Kingdom for use in Europe.

AN LST ARRIVES IN PLYMOUTH, England, carrying an LCT(6) as deckload, after crossing the Atlantic under its own power (top). The LCT was unloaded by sliding it over the side of the LST into the water (bottom). A great many landing craft were needed to mount the coming invasion. These were built in the United States and the United Kingdom.

OUTDOOR STORAGE OF FIELD WIRE which was to be used after the invasion of France by the Signal Corps for telephone communications. The large rolls contained one mile of wire while the smaller ones had a half-mile capacity (top). The Quartermaster Corps, after salvaging shoes, supervised the rebuilding of them in English shoe factories and returned the remade shoes to troops in the field. Bottom picture shows shoes before and after being rebuilt.

MEN OF A QUARTERMASTER UNIT STORING FIELD RATIONS in a warehouse in England, March 1944 (top). The U. S. Army was unquestionably better fed than any other in history. However, food in combat can never be the same as that in garrison or cantonment, since field rations must be nonperishable, compact, and easily carried by the individual soldier. Combat rations were improved as the war progressed and C rations were supplied in a more varied assortment. Engineer construction supplies stored in England in preparation for the invasion of Normandy (bottom). The large rolls of wire netting were to be used on the invasion beaches to make improvised roadways for vehicles.

PARATROOPERS MAKING A MASS JUMP during their training in England. In practice jumps prior to the drop into Normandy there were numerous casualties. The injured were quickly cared for and the experience showed airborne medics what they could expect during the actual invasion.

REPUBLIC P–47 FIGHTER PLANES (top) and Boeing B–17 heavy bombers (bottom) lined up on an airfield in England before being issued to the units who will fly them over the Continent against the enemy.

ENGINEERS CONSTRUCTING A PONTON BRIDGE in England during the training period (top). Members of an antiaircraft artillery unit receiving instruction from a British officer while training with a 40-mm. automatic antiaircraft gun M1 (bottom).

GUN CREW OF AN ANTIAIRCRAFT ARTILLERY GROUP operating a
90-mm. gun M1 near the coast of England, April 1944. In order to cope with the
latest developments in the fields of high-altitude bombing, a 90-mm. antiaircraft gun
with longer range, greater muzzle velocity, and a larger effective shell-burst area was
introduced.

EXHAUST STACKS AND AIR-INTAKE VENTS being installed on a medium tank M4 (top). After the installation was completed, the tank was tested off the coast of England (bottom). In addition to stacks, the tanks were further waterproofed by sealing all unvented openings with tape and sealing compound to render the hull watertight. Special attachments permitted rapid jettisoning of any waterproofing equipment which might interfere with satisfactory operation of the vehicles when on shore. These methods were first successfully used in the invasion of North Africa in November 1942. All vehicles which were to be driven ashore in Normandy under their own power, through water, and in the face of enemy fire, were waterproofed. Ordnance inspectors checked the vehicle in the marshalling yards a few hours before the tanks were loaded for the invasion.

LCT(R) FIRING ROCKETS DURING A TEST in Portsmouth Harbor, England (top). Close-up of the rocket launchers (bottom). These ships converted from landing craft, tank, were equipped to fire as many as 1,000 rockets.

LANDING MANEUVERS. During late April and early May 1944 these were held for the invasion troops. Infantrymen landing from an LCI(L) (top). A combination gun motor carriage M15A1 landing on the beach from an LCT (bottom). This was a highly mobile weapon, capable of a concentration of rapid fire, and designed for antiaircraft defense.

WATERPROOFED TANK RECOVERY VEHICLE M31 being loaded on an LCT during training along the English coast (top). For camouflage purposes, the normal appearance of the tank was retained as far as possible. A simulated turret without cupola was used and dummy 75-mm. and 37-mm. guns were mounted in place of the real guns. Actual armament was limited to two .30-caliber machine guns. A half-track 81-mm. mortar carrier M21 maneuvering on a road in England (bottom). The mortar could be used on the vehicle or separate from it.

BOAT-LANDING DRILL during a training exercise, Slapton Sands near Weymouth, Devon, England, May 1944. The infantrymen shown here have their equipment as complete as it will be during the actual invasion landings. They are descending ladders into an LCVP. Standing with his back to the camera at the top of the ladder is an officer, identified by the broad white vertical stripe painted on the back of his helmet. Noncommissioned officers had a similar horizontal stripe painted on their helmets.

**MEN AND TRUCKS ON THE UPPER DECK OF AN LST** near Slapton Sands in May 1944. As D Day drew nearer loading exercises and amphibious operations were practiced by the invasion troops. The greatest advantage the United States was to have in equipment over the Germans was the multiple-drive motor equipment, principally the 1/4-ton truck and the 2 1/2-ton truck. Shown in the picture are: 1/4-ton 4x4 truck, 3/4-ton 4x4 weapons carrier truck, 1 1/2-ton 6x6 personnel and cargo truck, and 2 1/2-ton 6x6 truck.

AMPHIBIAN TRUCKS CARRY SUPPLIES ASHORE from a coaster under the protection of a smoke screen during landing maneuvers (top). A 2½-ton amphibian truck hitting the beach during maneuvers (bottom). These versatile trucks proved invaluable in bringing supplies to the beaches during the early stages of landing and during the build-up after the invasion of Normandy. During one of the amphibious exercises, which were made as realistic as possible, two LST's were sunk by German E-boats. In other respects the training was successful and valuable lessons were learned.

LCVP'S CIRCLING NEAR THE MOTHER SHIP while waiting for the signal to land on the beach during landing operation training at Slapton Sands (top). Members of an armored unit being briefed at a marshalling area (bottom). At the conclusion of the training exercises in May all the assault, follow-up, and build-up troops moved from their camps to marshalling areas for final staging.

MEN AND EQUIPMENT BEING LOADED INTO LST'S (top) and LCVP's (bottom) during the first days of June 1944 at one of the "hards" (paved strips running to the water's edge) in southern England for the invasion of Normandy. The training given the assault forces during the amphibious exercises was so thorough that the final loadings for the invasion were accomplished with a minimum of delay and confusion and resembled another exercise more than the real thing. Two and one-half years after the first U. S. troops sailed for the United Kingdom, the training and preparation was completed and the large invasion force of U. S. and Allied troops was to receive its real test in battle against the enemy.

# NORMANDY CAMPAIGN

The American and British

Invasion Beaches

and the Allied Advance

during   the

Normandy Campaign

6 June 1944 to 24 July 1944

# Normandy Campaign[*]

On 6 June 1944 the Allied military forces invaded northern France. After long study of the German strength, including coastal defenses and the disposition of enemy troops, the Allied commanders selected the beaches along the Bay of the Seine for the assault landings. The two beaches to be used by troops of the First U. S. Army were given the names of UTAH and OMAHA. Those on which the British and Canadians of the British Second Army were to land were named GOLD, SWORD, and JUNO. The assault began at 0200 on 6 June when airborne troops were dropped behind the beaches with the mission of securing exits from the beaches. Planes of the Allied air force bombed the coastal defenses and shortly after sunrise the Navy began shelling the beach defenses. At 0630 the first troops landed on the beaches of Normandy. The sea was rough and the assault forces met varying degrees of enemy opposition, but the beachheads were secured and the assault and follow-up troops moved on to accomplish their missions. The U. S. forces landing on UTAH Beach moved northwest to clear the northern portion of the Cotentin Peninsula and capture the port of Cherbourg. Those landing on OMAHA Beach advanced southward toward Saint-Lô. The troops of the British Second Army were to advance in a southeast direction from Caen.

The enormous build-up of men and material began immediately after the assault. This operation was made most difficult because of the lack of port facilities, but before the invasion plans had been made for the construction of artificial harbors. The plans were quickly put into effect and the harbors were almost completed when a summer gale struck the Channel coast destroying most of the construction work. By using amphibian trucks and Rhino ferries, and by drying out LST's, the build-up over open beaches progressed much faster than was anticipated and men and supplies were poured into France in ever increasing numbers.

---

[*] See Roland P. Ruppenthal, Break-Out and Pursuit, now in preparation for the series U. S. Army in World War II.

While the beachheads were expanded and the build-up continued, the infantry and armored units fought their way through the hedgerow country toward their objectives. The fighting was slow and costly as enemy opposition stiffened in an unsuccessful attempt to prevent the Allied advance. With the capture of Cherbourg and Saint-Lô the initial missions of the U. S. forces were completed and the forces were then assembled in preparation for the drives south and west from the beachhead toward Avranches and the Brittany Peninsula. The British forces were to push southward from Caen exploiting in the direction of Paris and the Seine Basin. These attacks were scheduled to begin on 19 July 1944 but because of bad weather the supporting aerial assault was delayed and the breakout of Normandy did not get under way until 25 July.

FULLY EQUIPPED PARATROOPER, armed with a Thompson submachine gun M1, climbing into a transport plane to go to France as the invasion of Normandy gets under way. At approximately 0200, 6 June 1944, men of two U. S. airborne divisions, as well as elements of a British airborne division, were dropped in vital areas to the rear of German coastal defenses guarding the Normandy beaches from Cherbourg to Caen. By dawn 1,136 heavy bombers of the RAF Bomber Command had dropped 5,853 tons of bombs on selected coastal batteries lining the Bay of the Seine between Cherbourg and Le Havre.

A MARTIN B–26 MEDIUM BOMBER flying over one of the invasion beaches, early on D-Day morning. All planes which supported the invasion operations, with the exception of the four-motored bombers, were painted with three white and two black stripes for identification purposes. At dawn on D Day the U. S. Air Forces took up the air attacks and in the half hour before the touchdown of the assault forces (from 0600 to 0630) 1,365 heavy bombers dropped 2,746 tons of high explosives on the shore defenses. This was followed by attacks by medium bombers, light bombers, and fighter bombers. During the 24 hours of 6 June Allied aircraft flew 13,000 sorties, and during the first 8 hours alone dropped 10,000 tons of bombs.

GUN CREW ALERT aboard the cruiser USS *Augusta,* as landing craft approach the coast of France during the invasion, 6 June 1944. The three landing craft nearest the *Augusta* are an LCT(6), an LBV, and an LBK. While the Allied air forces were bombing installations along the invasion beaches the Allied sea armada drew in toward the coast, preceded by its flotillas of mine sweepers. Bad weather conditions and high seas had driven the enemy surface patrol craft into their harbors, and the 100-mile movement across the English Channel was unopposed. By 0300 the ships had anchored in the transport areas some thirteen miles off their assigned beaches, and the loading of troops into landing craft and the forming of the assault waves for the dash to the beaches began. At 0550 the heavy naval support squadrons began a 45-minute bombardment which quickly silenced the major coast-defense batteries.

OMAHA BEACH ON 6 JUNE 1944. From Grandcamp, cliffs extend eastward to
Arromanches-les-Bains with only two breaks, one in the Vierville–Colleville region
which was the V Corps area. The Aure River behind OMAHA Beach is a serious
obstacle for a distance of ten miles from its mouth, near Isigny. Between the Vire and
Orne Rivers the area is covered to a depth of forty miles inland by bocage (land divided

into small fields by hedges, banks, and sunken roads). Observation was limited, and vehicle movement was restricted to the roads. The highlands that extend across the invasion front, with a depth up to twenty-five miles, are broken with steep hills and narrow valleys. Although narrow, the roads in this area are generally good. Vital initial objectives were the towns of Carentan, Saint-Lô, Bayeux, and Caen.

**U. S. TROOPS WADING ASHORE FROM AN LCVP** at Omaha Beach during the assault. Elements of two U. S. infantry divisions, with engineer troops and tanks of an armored unit, made the first landings. The beaches selected for these landings were about 7,000 yards in length. From the beach the ground curves upward and is backed by bluffs that merge into the cliffs at either end of the sector. H Hour was at 0630 6 June. The mission of V Corps was to secure a beachhead in the area between the Vire River and Port-en-Bessin, from which troops would push southward toward Caumont and Saint-Lô, conforming to the advance of British Second Army to the east.

INFANTRYMEN WADING ASHORE FROM AN LCT(6) (top). Troops leaving an LCVP to wade ashore (bottom). Half-tracks and 2½-ton amphibian trucks can be seen on the beach, and in the background men marching in columns start southward toward the bluffs. On the shelf the enemy strung barbed wire and planted mines. Lanes had to be cleared through these obstacles before the infantry could advance. Beyond this strip containing obstacles, the enemy laid out firing positions to cover the tidal flat and the beach with direct fire, both plunging and grazing, from all types of weapons. The men landing were fired upon from these positions, which for the most part had escaped destruction during the prelanding bombardment.

SURVIVORS OF AN LCVP which sank off OMAHA Beach coming ashore in an LCR(S). The high seas added to the difficulties in getting ashore. Landing craft were in some instances hurled onto the beaches by the waves and some of the smaller ones were swamped before reaching shore. Others were flung upon and holed by the mined underwater obstacles. Some of the assault troops were swept off their feet while wading through the breakers. Of these some were drowned and those who reached the beach were often near exhaustion. Because of the rough seas many of the men were seasick during the crossing and arrived on the beach with their combat efficiency temporarily impaired by the experience.

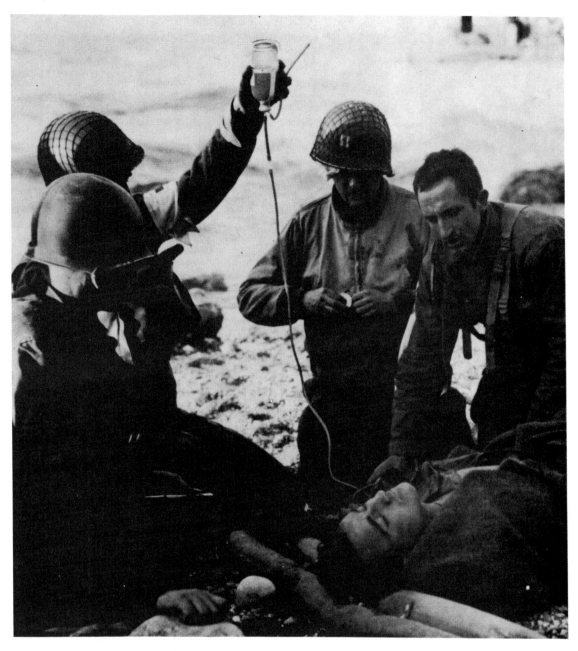

ARMY MEDICS ADMINISTERING BLOOD PLASMA to a survivor of a sunken landing craft on OMAHA Beach. D-Day casualties for the V Corps were in the neighborhood of 3,000 killed, wounded, and missing. The two assaulting regimental combat teams lost about 1,000 men each. The highest proportionate losses were taken by units that landed in the first few hours, including engineers, tank troops, and artillerymen. The D-Day casualties of V Corps were much higher than those suffered by VII Corps, where the assaulting seaborne division lost 197 men, including 60 lost at sea.

WOUNDED U. S. TROOPS OF V CORPS, waiting to be evacuated, take shelter under the cliffs near the beach in the Colleville area (top). Some German troops and laborers rounded up on OMAHA Beach (bottom). The assault troops reached the line of the Bayeux–Carentan road on 7 June. The following day U. S. forces established contact with the British on the American left flank. On 9 June U. S. divisions advanced rapidly south and west reaching the Caumont–Forêt de Cerisy–Isigny line by 11 June.

MEMBERS OF A SHORE FIRE CONTROL GROUP operating Signal Corps radios. Man at left is operating an SCR 284, while the second man operates the hand generator GN 45; man at right is using a hand-held radio set, "handie-talkie" SCR 536 (top).   An enlisted man looks up a number before placing a telephone call on a field telephone EE 8 (bottom). The function of the Signal Corps was to furnish radio, wire, and messenger communications. Often Signal Corps personnel went inland, sometimes ahead of the infantry, to observe and correct the fire from the naval guns offshore.

UTAH BEACH, 6 JUNE 1944. In the VII Corps zone the smooth and shallow beaches in the vicinity of Saint-Martin-de-Varreville are backed by sand dunes that extend inland 150 to 1,000 yards. Behind the sand dunes the low ground had been inundated for a width of one to two miles, restricting travel from the beaches to four easily defended causeways. Farther inland the Merderet River, running parallel to

the coast, and the Douve River, from which the ground rises northward to the hills around Cherbourg, restrict traffic to the established roads. Sainte-Mère-Eglise, Saint-Sauveur, and Barneville are key points on the road nets leading to Cherbourg. Southeast of UTAH Beach the Douve and Vire Rivers flow into the shallow, muddy Carentan estuary which marked the boundary between VII and V Corps.

ASSAULT TROOPS LANDING ON UTAH BEACH ON D DAY (top). Men and equipment along UTAH Beach on D Day (bottom). The mission of VII Corps was to assault UTAH Beach on 6 June 1944 at H Hour, 0630, and to capture Cherbourg with a minimum delay. The troops, landing just west of the Vire estuary, encountered less opposition than any other Allied forces on D Day.

INFANTRYMEN RESTING ALONG THE SEA WALL and beginning to move inland, 6 June (top). Advancing southward through the inundated low ground (bottom). Fortunately, the first elements landed considerably south of the designated beaches in areas less thickly obstructed and where enemy shore defenses were less formidable than those opposite the intended landing beaches. While airborne troops seized the causeways through the inundated low ground to prevent enemy reinforcements from reaching the beach, the seaborne assault troops struck northwest toward Montebourg, on the road to Cherbourg.

AN ENEMY SHELL HITS THE BEACH where U. S. troops are advancing.

GERMAN CASEMATED FORTIFICATION inland from the beach (top); destroyed enemy gun emplacement (bottom). During 1943 the Germans had developed heavy frontal defenses at all the principal harbors from Den Helder to Brest. As the invasion threat grew, Cherbourg and Le Havre were further strengthened, while heavy guns were installed to block the entrance of the Bay of the Seine. Between the ports stretched a line of concrete defense positions and coastal and flak batteries. A program of casemating the coastal guns and strengthening the defense posts was still in progress on 6 June. The beaches were mined and obstacles were placed in the water offshore and on the beaches, but there was no secondary defense line behind the coastal defenses which the Germans thought would stop the invading troops.

MEMBERS OF THE FOLLOW-UP DIVISION aboard an LCI(L) headed for
UTAH Beach on D Day. Other LCI's in the background have barrage balloons flying
overhead. These balloons were attached by cables to ships crossing the Channel so as
to keep low-flying enemy strafing planes away from the craft.

A MEMBER OF AN ENGINEER UNIT using a mine detector SCR 625. The ground outlined with white tape had not been cleared of enemy mines and enemy signs were used to mark the mined areas. Army and Navy demolition teams, following the assault infantry, found the beach less thickly obstructed than expected, and UTAH Beach was cleared in an hour. Engineers prepared exits from the beach by clearing lanes through the mine fields.

GLIDERS BEING TOWED BY C–47 TRANSPORTS over the English Channel carrying reinforcements for the airborne divisions, 7 June (top). A British Horsa glider wrecked while landing (bottom). Six thousand six hundred men of one of the two U. S. airborne divisions were scattered over an area 25 miles by 15 miles in extent, and 60 percent of their equipment was lost. In general, however, these men accomplished their mission successfully. Other gliders were flown in on 6 June but suffered considerable casualties. (CG4A WACO.)

GLIDERS AND TOW PLANES CIRCLING before the gliders are cut loose for a landing, 7 June. On the ground are gliders which landed the previous day, many of which were wrecked in landing. While one airborne division of the U. S. forces held the exits to Utah Beach and struck southward toward Carentan, the other airborne division, despite heavy shelling in the Sainte-Mère-Eglise area, also established contact with the infantry troops pushing inland from Utah Beach early on 7 June.

AN LCT(5) LOADED WITH REINFORCEMENTS moving toward the beach on 7 June. In left center is an LCT(R); at right center is an LBV. In the background supply ships wait to discharge their cargoes (top). U. S. Air Force glider pilots in an LCVP on their way to a larger ship which will take them back to England (bottom). After landing their gliders the pilots made their way to the beach to await shipping to return them to their bases.

AMPHIBIAN TRUCKS (DUKW's) bring supplies ashore on UTAH Beach, 8 June (top). Men and supplies come ashore; on the beach are LCT's (bottom). Between 7 and 12 June the Allies concentrated their efforts on joining the beachheads into one uninterrupted lodgement area and on bringing in men and supplies.

A RAILROAD BRIDGE ACROSS THE SEINE destroyed by bombers of the Allied air force. Even though hampered by poor flying weather during the first week after D Day, the Allied air force bombed bridges across the Seine and Loire Rivers. This seriously hindered the movement of enemy troops and supplies, and trains had to be constantly rerouted in an attempt to reinforce the Germans trying to hold the assault forces in the area of the beachheads.

WRECKED TRAIN. Three trains were held up on this single track, in the vicinity of Chartres, when fighter bombers knocked cars off the track. With the track thus blocked the movement of trains was stopped and much of the undamaged rolling stock later fell into Allied hands. Within an arc extending from the Pas-de-Calais through Paris to the Brittany Peninsula, 16,000 tons of bombs were dropped on coastal batteries, 4,000 tons on airfields, and 8,500 tons on railway targets between 6 and 11 June.

AURE RIVER

TRÉVIÈRES AND THE SURROUNDING AREA showing the bocage type of terrain. U. S. forces advancing inland from the OMAHA beachhead were checked by the enemy in the Formigny–Trévières area on 7 June. Formigny was cleared on 8 June. On the same day the U. S. troops held their positions north and east of Trévières and patrolled the outskirts of the town. The town was shelled by navy guns

in the late afternoon. The approach to Trévières from the high ground just north of the Aure River was strongly defended and the enemy forces continued to hold out in this area until 10 June when the attacking U. S. forces outflanked and captured the town. The fall of Trévières marked the end of enemy resistance north of the Forêt de Cerisy.

U. S. GUN CREW FIRING A 3-INCH ANTITANK GUN M5 at a house in
which enemy troops are holding out (top). In the advance of the Allies from UTAH
Beach toward Cherbourg the enemy was often cut off in small groups and surrounded.
The enemy groups in many cases would refuse to surrender, even though they were
cut off from their own forces, and had to be eliminated one group at a time. A 90-mm.
gun M1 of an antiaircraft battery firing near Vierville (bottom). Though enemy air
attacks were not a serious threat to the Allies and very little opposition was encountered, antiaircraft batteries were always on the alert.

MULTIPLE GUN MOTOR CARRIAGE M16 with its four .50-caliber machine guns firing at the enemy in support of an infantry advance (top). This vehicle was a weapon of an antiaircraft artillery unit, but the lack of enemy air activity in Normandy made possible its use in other roles. U. S. artillerymen emplacing a 155-mm. howitzer M1 in a camouflaged position (bottom).

FORMATION OF DOUGLAS A-20's over France. The infantry and armored attacks were, when possible, preceded by concentrated air attacks. Employing carpet bombing methods, thousands of tons of bombs were dropped. Fragmentation bombs were used to break enemy resistance without causing extensive cratering which would hinder the advance of tanks. Although these attacks were temporary in effect, the results greatly aided the initial ground attack. Casualties to the enemy were few, but he was stunned by the weight of the bombing and considerable confusion ensued.

ENGINEERS LAYING WIRE MATTING in the construction of a landing strip near Sainte-Mère-Eglise (top). A Republic P–47 Thunderbolt bursting into flames after crash landing on the strip; still attached to underside of the wing are rockets which were not fired (bottom). An important factor in insuring the success of the Allied close-support operations lay in the establishment of landing strips in Normandy, from which fighter planes could operate. Work began as soon as a footing was obtained on shore and by 9 June planes were operating from these strips.

A QUARRY NEAR OMAHA BEACH used by engineer units to supply rock and stone for the construction of roads. The tremendous amount of traffic on the roads in Normandy, as men and supplies were brought into France over the beaches, required the services of many engineer units to keep the roads in good repair. Most of the roads leading to the beaches were not hard surfaced but were constructed of rock and gravel.

ENLISTED MEN PREPARE TO LAUNCH A BARRAGE BALLOON over one of the beaches in Normandy. Balloons were attached to cables and by means of winches could be raised or lowered to the desired altitude. These balloons were used to protect ships and beach installations from low-flying enemy aircraft. When the balloons were in position the enemy would not fly low over the beaches for fear of running into the cables which kept the balloons in place.

**MEDICAL CORPS MEN TREATING AN ENLISTED MAN** for a wrist wound. When casualties entered a battalion aid station within a few hundred yards of the front, they were immediately screened and sorted. Wounds were redressed, and perhaps morphine or other drugs were given when available. Those whose wounds permitted were evacuated to the rear, while those whose wounds did not permit further evacuation were held, treated, given plasma, and then moved farther back.

AN EVACUATION HOSPITAL with a 750-bed capacity, Normandy, 24 July (top). Army surgeons perform an operation out-of-doors (bottom). In World War II the number of deaths per hundred casualties was one half of that during World War I. Responsible for this reduction was the surgical skill and painstaking care rendered by personnel of the Medical Corps aided by better surgery, the sulfa drugs, penicillin, plasma, and whole blood.

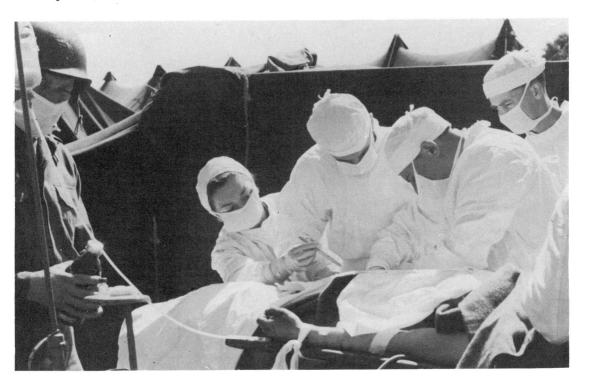

ENEMY PRISONERS, taken during the first days of fighting, awaiting transportation to England. During the first week following the invasion landings the Germans lost some 10,000 men as prisoners. The enemy forces that manned the static beach defenses were largely Russians and other non-Germans, but were under German officers. Of the German troops, many companies were found to be composed of men either under 20 or over 45 years of age. Many of these were of low medical categories and their morale was not of the best.

A MILITARY POLICEMAN studying French aboard a transport while waiting for the landing craft which will carry him to the beach in Normandy. In addition to handling informational and recreational activities of all kinds, the Special Services Division of the Army Service Forces distributed pocket-sized soldier guides to the customs and languages of the countries where members of the armed forces served. The Army, recognizing that the strain created by war must be counteracted by healthy diversional activities, arranged motion pictures and USO shows, and distributed books, magazines, and athletic and other recreational equipment to members and units of the armed forces.

VIRE-TAUTE CANAL

CARENTAN. The approach to Carentan from the east is blocked by the Vire-Taute Canal. U. S. forces advancing to secure the bridge on the road from Isigny met with enemy resistance from the houses and hedgerows on the east bank and it was not until midnight of 10 June that the enemy was driven out and defensive positions were

BASIN

established by U. S. troops. Other U. S. troops moved along the Bassin à Flot and crossed the canal on 12 June, moving rapidly into the center of Carentan which by then was ringed by attacking troops. This trap was closed too late to capture most of the German defenders, who escaped to the south during the night of 11–12 June.

U. S. TROOPS MOVING INTO CARENTAN, 12 June (top). A 105-mm. howitzer M3 firing at enemy positions during the fighting at Carentan (bottom). During the night of 11–12 June, Carentan was set ablaze by artillery and naval gunfire, and early on the morning of 12 June U. S. troops entered the town. Its fall marked the effective junction of the two U. S. beachheads and the linking up of the two corps of the First U. S. Army.

U. S. PARATROOPERS PATROLLING THE STREETS OF CARENTAN in a captured German *Volkswagen* (*1. Pkw. K. 1* (*typ 82*)) (top). Airborne troops in a jeep towing a British 6-pounder Mark III antitank gun in Carentan (bottom). The enemy counterattacks against the U. S. forces in Carentan were unsuccessful in their attempts to recapture the city, but were persistent enough to limit the U. S. advance to gains measured in hundreds of yards. However, on 17 June 1944 U. S. troops reached the west coast in the vicinity of Barneville, cutting the German forces into two groups, one south of the Carentan–Barneville line, the other in the Cherbourg area.

DOUGLAS A–20'S DROPPING BOMBS on a probable flying bomb launching site. The first flying bombs fell on England during the night of 12–13 June 1944, and the regular attacks began three days later. The smallness, the effective nature of camouflage, the comparative mobility, and the ease with which the V–1 launching sites could be repaired made effective bombing attacks on them difficult.

PART OF A GERMAN ROCKET INSTALLATION captured by U. S. troops.
Many of these flying bomb sites were captured by the Allies as they advanced.
Although the air force had destroyed some by bombing, most of the sites were taken
by advancing troops and destroyed.

A PORTION OF THE ARTIFICIAL HARBOR AT OMAHA BEACH. This harbor was in the Saint-Laurent-sur-Mer area of OMAHA Beach and was known as "MULBERRY A." Breakwaters were formed by sinking ships and concrete caissons, and steel bridging formed causeways to the beach. The harbor, construction on which began on 7 June 1944, was designed to provide moorings for seven Liberty ships and twelve coasters at one time. By 19 June it was 90 percent completed.

ENGINEERS LAYING STEEL MATTING on OMAHA Beach at the exits of the causeway which extend to the piers of the artificial harbor (top). Vehicles moving from one of the piers over the causeway to the shore (bottom). These floating causeways to the beach rose and fell with the tide. The artificial harbors were constructed to facilitate the unloading of the large numbers of men and material.

DAMAGE TO THE ARTIFICIAL HARBOR AND LANDING CRAFT caused by the storm. The greatest detriment to the Allied build-up was not the enemy, but the weather. From 19–22 June 1944 one of the worst summer gales in Channel history hit the Bay of the Seine. Unloading operations were virtually stopped, the floating steel caissons broke free and sank, the concrete caissons moved or were broken up, and the beach was strewn with hundreds of stranded and damaged craft. The line of sunken ships remained fairly well intact, but as a whole the artificial harbor was destroyed and useless.

A TRUCK ON THE BEACH (2½-ton) and one starting down the ramp of an LST (1½-ton). After the storm wrecked the artificial harbors emergency measures, such as using 2½-ton amphibian trucks to bring men and supplies ashore and "drying out" landing ships and coasters, were employed. By "drying out" the vessels (as in picture) and unloading directly on the beaches, unloading operations were carried out.

TRUCKS FULLY LOADED with men and supplies leaving a Rhino ferry and being helped ashore by a bulldozer (top). A ¾-ton weapons carrier rolling through the surf toward the beach under its own power (bottom). All the vehicles which made these landings through the surf had been waterproofed before leaving England. Since they were able to travel only a short distance on land under their own power when waterproofed, the waterproofing material was removed soon after the vehicles landed.

TRUCKS AND AMPHIBIAN TRUCKS (each is a 2½-ton truck) on a beach in Normandy. In spite of the damage caused by the storm, by 26 June OMAHA Beach was discharging 122 percent of its planned cargo capacity. By this time 268,718 men, 40,191 vehicles, and 125,812 tons of cargo had been discharged over OMAHA Beach alone. By 1 July the Allied commanders were not as much worried about a German counterattack that would threaten the beachhead as about the possibility that the enemy might bring in sufficient reserves to create a stalemate in Normandy. More room was needed by the Allies to bring in men and supplies to support a sustained drive toward the Seine.

UNIT ADVANCING TOWARD CHERBOURG stops to inspect a German multi-purpose gun (8.8-cm. *Flak*). When the enemy retreated from the vicinity of Monte-bourg he destroyed the gun by splaying the barrel. This multipurpose weapon emerged as the most publicized artillery piece of the German Army during the North African campaign. It was primarily an antiaircraft gun adaptable to antitank and general artillery use. In its role as an antitank gun it was fitted with a shield. In its mobile form it was towed on four wheels, usually with an 8-ton half-tracked tractor.

RESULTS OF ARTILLERY FIRE AND BOMBINGS in Montebourg (top). A 155-mm. howitzer M1 firing on the defenses of the city of Cherbourg (bottom). On 19 June Montebourg fell to the U. S. forces and Valognes was taken the following day. The advance on Cherbourg was continued by three U. S. infantry divisions. An attack on Cherbourg was launched on the afternoon of 22 June, after an 80-minute air and artillery bombardment of the outer defenses, but the enemy at first fought back with determination.

HILL 171 AREA                    BOIS DU MONT DU ROC

THE BOIS DU MONT DU ROC AREA. On 22–23 June the U. S. troops launched an attack from the valley to seize Hill 171. The critical enemy defense areas at Flottemanville-Hague and Hill 171 were closely pressed and before dark on 23 June the area of Hill 171 was reached and 400 enemy prisoners were taken. The Flotte-manville-Hague defenses were bombed by Allied planes and the defenses were taken by the ground forces shortly thereafter. The enemy's fortified line protecting Cherbourg was then broken and the U. S. troops were ready for the final drive to the city.

FORTIFICATIONS AROUND CHERBOURG DAMAGED by Allied shelling and bombardment. The German defenders refused to surrender the city to the attacking U. S. forces, and on 22 June a co-ordinated attack was launched by the attackers, supported by aircraft of the tactical air forces and heavy artillery fire. However, no real break-through was achieved by this bombardment and the U. S. troops resorted to the methodical reduction of the strong points. It was not until 24 June that the main defenses cracked, and the next day the three attacking infantry divisions, supported by heavy naval bombardment, reached the outskirts of the city.

TWO U. S. INFANTRYMEN ROUTING A SNIPER during street fighting in Cherbourg (top). German prisoners taken in Cherbourg (bottom). By 25 June U. S. forces were fighting in the streets of the city while the Germans demolished the port facilities. At 1500 on 26 June the German commanders surrendered. The Arsenal held out until the following morning and fanatical groups had to be eliminated one by one. A certain number of the enemy still remained to be rounded up in the north-west corner of the Cotentin Peninsula, but on 1 July all resistance in the northern Cotentin came to an end.

A MEMBER OF AN ENGINEER UNIT, operating a bulldozer, clears a street in Cherbourg (top). Members of an Engineer unit stationed in Cherbourg take time out to prepare a meal in the doorway of a house (bottom). C and K rations were generally issued to troops in combat. Where there was more time for the preparation of food, troops were given the "10 in 1" ration which contained more variety than the C and K rations. When units were more permanently settled regular messes were set up, but during the early days on the Continent just after the invasion, and while the supply situation was still critical, troops resorted to eating rations that could be more easily transported and prepared.

FORT DU ROULE          ARSENAL AREA

A PORTION OF CHERBOURG showing the inner harbor and docks. Fort du Roule, built high and secure into a steep rock promontory which stands immediately back of the city, dominated the entire harbor area. It was primarily a coastal fortress but was also defended against a ground attack. The P–47's which bombed the fort did little damage to the subterranean tunnels housing the big guns. The fort was finally taken by infantry troops armed with machine guns, mortars, grenades, pole charges,

and rifles. The fort surrendered in sections and it was not until late on 25 June that the complete surrender was accomplished. After the rest of the city had been taken the Arsenal still held out. This structure, partially protected by a moat, was high-walled and well-armed. On 27 June the Arsenal surrendered bringing to an end all organized resistance in the city. With the fall of the city every effort was made to clear the harbor and repair docking facilities as quickly as possible.

THE FIRST SHIP-TO-SHORE GASOLINE LINE, put in operation at Cherbourg. During the assault phase the Allied forces relied on canned gasoline, but by 3 July bulk supply was being introduced by ship-to-shore pipeline which brought in part of the large quantities of gasoline necessary to the Allied forces.

ORDNANCE MEN CUTTING ANGLE-IRON with acetylene torches (top). An M5 light tank equipped with a hedgerow cutter (bottom). During the fighting in Normandy armored vehicles found the hedgerows a serious obstacle which they could neither cross over nor break through. An enlisted man of an Ordnance unit in Normandy devised the method of attaching to the front of tanks rake-like cutters improvised from heavy angle-iron salvaged from the underwater beach obstacles which the Germans had placed to wreck landing craft. During a period of 48 hours maintenance companies of the Ordnance Department turned out 300 of these cutters, which enabled the tanks to open passageways through the hedgerows of Normandy, and play an important part in the advance leading to the break-through at Saint-Lô.

.30-CALIBER BROWNING MACHINE GUN M1919A4 being fired through an opening in a hedgerow by an infantryman. The July offensive, one of the most difficult and bloody phases of the Normandy Campaign and known as the Battle of the Hedgerows, was conducted from 7 to 20 July 1944. Four U. S. Army corps, ultimately employing twelve divisions, were involved in the effort. German reinforcements stiffened, particularly in the hills protecting Saint-Lô, and the U.S. forces in the Cotentin Peninsula fought their way southward, alongside the U.S. troops east of the Vire River, to win ground for mounting the attack which was to break through the German defenses at the end of the month of July.

A 3-INCH GUN MOTOR CARRIAGE M10 moving along a road near Saint-Fromond. While the British Second Army battled furiously against enemy armored strength to the east, the First U. S. Army struggled forward on both sides of the Vire River in their drive on Saint-Lô. The advance was laborious because of the nature of the terrain and the poor weather conditions. The enemy rallied to prevent any break-through to Saint-Lô, and the British redoubled their efforts in the Caen area where the Germans had most of their 900 tanks.

TWO GERMAN PANTHERS, heavy tanks (*Pz. Kpfw.*–7.5-cm. *Kw. K. 42–L/70*), knocked out on a road near Le Désert (top). A damaged German self-propelled assault gun (*Stu. G. IV* with *Stu. K. 40–L/48*) near Périers (bottom). During the fighting in the Saint-Lô area the German forces included two corps with elements of no less than twelve divisions, including two armored divisions. The losses sustained by the enemy armored units removed the possibility of a further large-scale counterattack west of the Vire River.

GERMAN PANTHER (top). U. S. medium tanks M4A1 pass German medium tanks (*Pz. Kpfw. IV*) which were knocked out in the July fighting near Saint-Lô (bottom). In hedgerow fighting tanks were expected to give great assistance, by their fire power, in dealing with hedgerow strong points but there was always the problem of getting them through the embankments fast enough to maintain their support to the infantry.

ARMY MEDICAL AID MEN preparing to evacuate wounded (top). U. S. troops along a sunken road during the advance to Saint-Lô (bottom). The U. S. losses during this campaign totaled nearly 11,000 killed, wounded, and missing. The Germans, as a result of the action, were prevented from regrouping and wore down their last immediate reserves for use against a break-through.

AN INFANTRY PATROL picking its way through the blasted ruins of Saint-Lô (top). Allied and German shelling and Allied aerial bombing reduced Saint-Lô to ruins (bottom). The original objectives of the July offensive were not attained except for the capture of Saint-Lô on 18 July 1944 and the high ground suitable for launching the break-through attempt. The ground won was sufficient to give the troops more room and better jump-off positions which they needed to break out of Normandy.

SAINT-LÔ IN RUINS after the capture of the city by the U. S. forces. It was shelled
both by the attacking Allied forces who needed the area to stage troops who were to

break out of the hedgerow country of Normandy, and by the enemy forces who were trying to prevent the U. S. troops from taking the city.

INFANTRYMEN RESTING IN THEIR FOXHOLE. Rain, which continued for 6 days, delayed the air bombardment and in turn the advance of the First Army which had scheduled an attack for 19 July 1944. During this period the men were compelled to huddle in their foxholes under the dripping hedgerows in conditions of extreme discomfort, while the enemy, also entrenched behind the natural defenses of the country, was alert to every movement. The low-lying country became a sea of mud, stopping further tank operations during this period.

JEEP SPLASHING THROUGH A FLOODED ROAD IN NORMANDY. The rains, which held up the advance, flooded the dirt roads which by this time were in a bad state of repair from the heavy traffic and shelling. On the front of the jeep is an iron bar used to cut thin strands of wire that the enemy strung across the roads level with the heads of the occupants of vehicles, which traveled with tops and windshields down.

INFANTRYMEN FIRING FROM A HEDGEROW. The man in the foreground is shown about to fire a fragmentation grenade using a U. S. rifle .30-calibre M1 with a grenade launcher M7 (top). Grenade has just been fired (bottom). The terrain through which the Allied troops fought was favorable to the defense. In the close bocage countryside, dotted with woods and orchards and with fields divided by tree-topped embankments where armor could not well be employed, the infantry had to wage a grim struggle from hedgerow to hedgerow and from bank to bank, harassed by snipers and machine gun posts. On 24 July the troops of the U. S. First Army were waiting for the weather to clear sufficiently for an air attack before they attempted to break out of Normandy in the area of the Périers–Lessay–Saint-Lô road.

# NORTHERN FRANCE
# CAMPAIGN

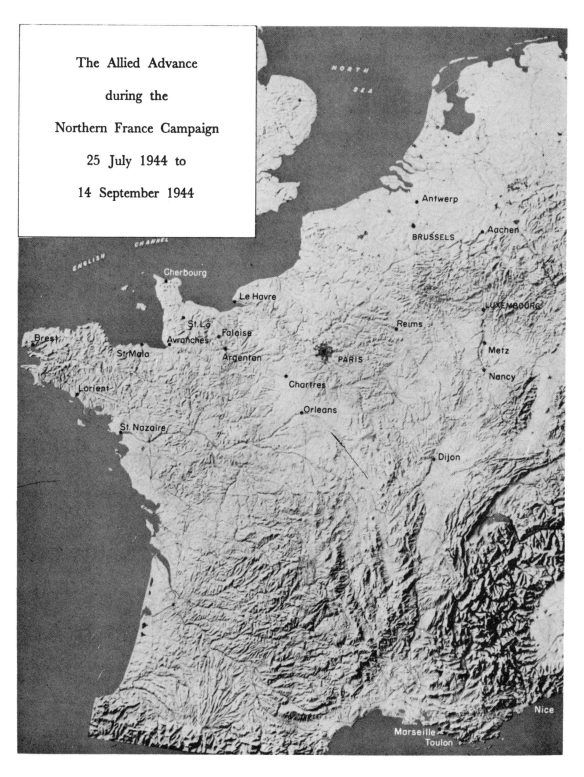

The Allied Advance

during the

Northern France Campaign

25 July 1944 to

14 September 1944

# Northern France Campaign *

On 25 July 1944 the Allied forces fighting in Normandy were able to begin the offensive to break out of Normandy and carry to the German frontier. Preceding the ground attack planes of the Allied air forces dropped more than 3,390 tons of bombs on enemy positions on a narrow front in the vicinity of Saint-Lô. The air attack's crushing power and its paralyzing effect on the German forces opened the way for a rapid and powerful drive by Allied armored and infantry units. Cities were captured in quick succession and the enemy troops were forced to flee in a disorderly retreat.

The armored spearheads led the way out the Brittany Peninsula which was quickly occupied, with the exception of the fortresses of the port cities which were to continue to fight until after the German borders had been reached. While part of the U. S. forces were overrunning the Brittany Peninsula, the major portion turned toward the east in the direction of Paris, and British and Canadian troops moved southward from Caen along the road to Falaise. The battle of the Falaise–Argentan pocket was a disastrous defeat for the German forces who were trying to prevent the Allies from moving eastward. During the fighting in this area elements of two German armies were so disorganized and destroyed that their effectiveness was greatly impaired.

Paris surrendered on 25 August and by the 27th all enemy resistance ceased there. The advance continued toward the eastern borders of France, where the Allies stopped their rapid drive, and though a few further advances were made, 14 September 1944 found them consolidating their positions along the Moselle River and northward in Belgium and Holland. The major port cities of Le Havre and Antwerp, which were badly needed by the Allies as ports of entry for men and materials, were captured.

---

*See Roland P. Ruppenthal, Break-Out and Pursuit.

During the Northern France Campaign the expanding Allied forces reorganized. The Supreme Headquarters, Allied Expeditionary Force, moved to the Continent of Europe. The 21 Army Group was made up of the British Second and the Canadian First Armies. The 12th Army Group, composed of the First and Third U. S. Armies, became operational. In August 1944 Allied forces invaded southern France and moved northward to join those in northern France. This force, made up of the U. S. Seventh and French First Armies, made a junction with the northern group on 11 September. Also during this period the U. S. Ninth Army became operational and took over the reduction of the Brittany fortresses.

MEDIUM TANK M4A1, equipped with a hedgerow cutter, breaking through a hedgerow. The build-up was continuing generally as anticipated and the destruction of the enemy forces progressed. On 23 July 1944 the Canadian First Army became operational on the left flank of the Allied line. The Third U. S. Army had begun moving to the Cotentin Peninsula on 5 July and was proceeding on the right flank of the Allied line.

75-MM. HOWITZER MOTOR CARRIAGES M8, partially concealed by a hedge-row, preparing to fire on enemy positions near Marigny (top). M5 light tanks pass through the streets of Coutances (bottom). The first attack was launched on a narrow front across the Périers road west of Saint-Lô. This attack was supported by heavy artillery and aerial bombardment. While the spearhead units advanced in the direction of Coutances, the rest of the First U. S. Army was to exert strong pressure and harass any attempted enemy withdrawal. Marigny was taken on 26 July and, though the enemy resisted stubbornly while trying to keep a corridor open for the withdrawing German forces, Coutances fell on 28 July.

ENGINEERS WEARING CAMOUFLAGE SUITS clean out a street in Canisy (top). Infantry troops set up a 57-mm. antitank gun M1 (bottom). Advances south from Saint-Lô reached Tessy-sur-Vire on 28 July, while another attack farther east met with severe resistance in the vicinity of Forêt de Cerisy. In the British-Canadian sector the advance had been halted by a strong enemy belt of antitank guns, dug-in tanks, and mortars.

MAIL CALL AT THE FRONT (top). The receiving of mail was always an important morale factor and every effort was made to get it to the men as quickly as possible. Infantrymen reading German propaganda leaflets during a rest period (bottom). German planes dropped propaganda leaflets in an attempt to discourage the Allies in their advances. These had little effect on the troops and the advances continued with all possible speed.

PRISONERS TAKEN BY THE ALLIES during the early part of August. Many of the men of the enemy forces were non-Germanic, some were Russians or members of Russian units who had been captured by the Germans on the eastern front and sent to Normandy as part of the enemy defense units. As the enemy retreat began to degenerate into a disorderly rout many prisoners were taken, and on 28 July 4,500 were captured.

FRENCH WOMAN, returning to her home after the German withdrawal, passes
a knocked out self-propelled antitank gun (*Pz. Jaeg. 38* with 7.5-cm. *Pak. 40/3*).
Many of the civilians left their homes and towns during the fighting and returned after-
wards, often to find that they had lost their homes during the artillery shelling and
aerial bombing. However, in some cases the civilian population stayed in the towns
during the fighting.

MOTOR COLUMN ADVANCING ALONG A ROAD near Coutances. On 29
July U. S. armored divisions trapped an enemy column about seven miles southeast
of Coutances. Fighter bombers came in and attacked the closely jammed columns
of vehicles destroying 137 tanks and over 500 other vehicles.

AN ARMORED COLUMN led by a light armored car M8 stops for a few minutes during its advance to Avranches (top). An M4 medium tank moving through a street in Avranches (bottom). On 30 July an armored division closely followed by an infantry division closed in on Granville. Another armored division entered Avranches and secured two bridges across the Sée River. The break-through was completed by 31 July, the area between Granville and Avranches was cleared of enemy pockets of resistance, and the U. S. forces struck southward in the direction of Villedieu.

ARMORED VEHICLES FIRING ON ENEMY TROOPS during the advance southward (top). Tanks and trucks of a French armored division in the assembly area after landing and before starting south to join the U. S. forces (bottom). On 1 August 1944, as the U. S. forces poured around the crumpled German flank at Avranches, a major revision was effected in the organization of the Allied forces. The Third U. S. Army became operational and at the same time the 12th Army Group headquarters also became operational and assumed command of the First and Third U. S. Armies. The 21 Army Group was at this time made up of the British Second and the Canadian First Armies.

SÉE RIVER

**AVRANCHES AND THE SURROUNDING COUNTRY.** After the fall of the
city the Allied drive gained momentum and the advancing troops swept out of

Normandy. Turning toward the east and the west in two attacks, the Allies drove to the German frontier and the tip of the Brittany Peninsula.

AMMUNITION BEING UNLOADED at an Ordnance dump after it had been brought inland from the beach (top). During the advance of the Allies south following the breakout from Normandy a maximum effort was required to keep all the using units supplied with ammunition. Tankers of an armored unit reloading their .30-caliber ammunition belts during the drive southward (bottom).

A BULLDOZER (tractor, earth moving crawler, diesel) pulling a jeep from a crater (top). Engineers using a truck-mounted revolving crane swing a section of a treadway bridge into place over the Vire River near Pontfarcy (bottom).

INFANTRYMEN TAKING A BREAK, their M1's leaning against the wall of a destroyed building. The Third U. S. Army drove southward from Avranches on 1 August with the mission of clearing the Brittany Peninsula and securing the ports. The attacks were spearheaded by armored divisions against only scattered opposition and by 3 August Loudéac was reached, infantrymen were closing in on the fortress of Saint-Malo, armored units were striking toward Vannes and Nantes, and Rennes had been captured. The 21st Army Group and First U. S. Army met dogged enemy resistance, but Mortain was occupied by the latter.

AN INFANTRYMAN USING HIS HELMET AS A BASIN while washing at a town pump. The weather during this period was hot and dry; inland from the coast there was little fog. The advancing men took every opportunity during the rapid advances to stop for a quick wash.

AN M4A1 MEDIUM TANK rolls through a battered French village. After the rapid advances through the Brittany Peninsula, U. S. forces were left in front of the main port cities to contain the enemy. The Third U. S. Army turned eastward driving with strong armored forces on the general axis of Laval–Le Mans–Chartres. The terrain that would be encountered in a drive to the Seine would be favorable for the use of armor, and the weather was expected to be good. On 4 August Mayenne was captured and contact with First U. S. Army units was established. During the next five days the drive to the east continued for a distance of 85 miles and the cities of Angers and Le Mans were taken.

INFANTRYMEN FIGHTING IN HEDGEROWS near Mortain. Shortly after midnight on 7 August a German counterattack struck the U. S. infantry division in the area of Mortain. By morning, when the enemy had penetrated the First Army line some three or four miles, Allied aircraft equipped with rockets attacked the enemy. Three U. S. divisions were quickly shifted to the area and for the next three days a fierce battle raged as the Germans tried to cut the corridor through which the Third Army was advancing onto the plains of western France. On 11 August, Mortain was re-entered by the First Army.

U. S. ARTILLERY OBSERVATION POST near Barenton, between Mortain and Domfront. After the failure of the German counterattack in the vicinity of Mortain the only alternative for the enemy was to retreat, and a gradual withdrawal was made toward the Seine River. During this period two simultaneous battles were fought: one by First Army troops and those of 21 Army Group around the Falaise–Argentan pocket, the other by the Third Army which was driving hard to the Seine River.

INFANTRYMEN OF THE FIRST ARMY advancing in the vicinity of Sourdeval against the withdrawing enemy forces. The Canadian First Army advancing south-ward along the Caen–Falaise road was to join forces with the U. S. troops advancing eastward. The Germans put up a strong defense aganst the Allied troops advancing to encircle them.

AN M4 MEDIUM TANK, rolling into Dreux, passes a German antitank gun (7.5-cm. *Pak. 40*). On 14 August the Third Army was ordered to leave sufficient forces to hold Argentan and to take advantage of the enemy's disorganization by continuing the main advance to the east. Advances were made against Dreux, Chartres, and Orléans. On 15 August Dreux was captured and on 17 August the First Army took over at Argentan. On 18 August the Third Army forces swung north to seize crossings of the Seine River below Paris and to begin the deep encirclement of the German troops south of the river.

TWO TYPES OF U. S. TRACKED VEHICLES, each mounting a 105-mm. howitzer. 105-mm. howitzer motor carriage M7 (top); medium tank M4A3 with 105-mm. howitzer (bottom).

CONVOY CARRYING GASOLINE ALONG RED BALL HIGHWAY. These are 4–5-ton trucks (tractors) towing 2,000-gallon semitrailers (top). A 12-ton truck towing a 45-ton trailer loaded with ammunition, stops along Red Ball Highway (bottom). With the resistance offered by the retreating enemy at a minimum during this period, fuel was a more vital requisite than ammunition. Approximately a million gallons of gasoline were needed at the front every day to enable the armored columns to maintain their headlong rate of advance.

**MILITARY POLICEMAN DIRECTS TRAFFIC ON RED BALL HIGHWAY.**
The three essential supplies were food, ammunition, and gasoline, and to get these
to the armored spearheads as quickly as possible a system known as the Red Ball Ex-
press was instituted. By this, a circular one-way traffic route was established across
France from the beachheads to the fighting zone and back again. All civilian and local
military traffic was prohibited the use of the Red Ball Highway, and along it the
convoys swept at high speed day and night.

RAILROAD EQUIPMENT BEING UNLOADED FROM A SEATRAIN at Cherbourg. Motor convoys could not handle the vast quantities of supplies needed to maintain the Allied fighting forces and it was necessary to supplement these convoys with rail transportation. The first scheduled run was made between Cherbourg and Carentan on 11 July 1944, using mostly salvaged French equipment. As soon as the Cherbourg port facilities were sufficiently restored, equipment was brought over from England and put into service.

DESTROYED RAILROAD EQUIPMENT. So greatly had the French railroads suffered that over 900 locomotives and a third of the rolling stock used had to be supplied from Allied sources in England. In addition to replacing locomotives and cars, bridges had to be constructed, wrecked trains had to be cleared, and tracks had to be replaced. Damage by Allied bombings at every major junction and marshalling yard had to be repaired. These tasks fell to men of the Corps of Engineers and the Transportation Corps.

AN INFANTRYMAN ARMED WITH AN M1 RIFLE looks at two German rocket launchers left behind by the enemy (8.8-cm. *Racketenpanzerbuchse*). The German weapon was of larger caliber and was heavier than the U. S. rocket launcher but similar in appearance and operation.

SIGNAL CORPS MAN OPERATING A SWITCHBOARD BD71. This small switchboard weighed approximately fifty pounds, had six lines, and was used with headset HS30, ear plugs, and chest set microphone. The set was generally used by regiments and smaller units. When the break-through came at the end of July 1944 the speed of the advances imposed a heavy strain on the communications personnel. Spearhead units relied mostly on radio communications, but a line net of great complexity was required in the rear areas to cope with the amount of traffic involved. Civilian communications were of limited value because of the lack of maintenance during the years of war destruction, and within four months of D Day the Allies laid over 100,000 circuit miles of telephone line.

A PORTION OF THE CITY OF FALAISE which was occupied on 17 August by
Canadian First Army troops who had pushed down the Caen–Falaise road. This city
on the northeast corner of the Falaise pocket was on the north corner of the encirclement in which the German troops were trapped.

A PORTION OF THE CITY OF ARGENTAN, the southeast corner of the Falaise pocket. On 12 August the Third Army armored divisions were at Argentan and Ecouché with infantry divisions in support. The enemy struggled to escape from the pocket through the gap between Falaise and Argentan and concentrated on removing his armored units, leaving the infantry to hold off the Allies. A considerable part of eight armored divisions managed to escape from the closing Allied pincers but left behind a great proportion of their equipment. On 20 August the trap was closed on more than seven infantry divisions and parts of two armored divisions. By 22 August the enemy in the pocket had been eliminated.

INFANTRYMEN PICKING THEIR WAY THROUGH DEBRIS and rubble in Domfront in pursuit of the fleeing enemy. When the Falaise–Argentan pocket was closed, Allied divisions inside the pocket pressed in on the remnants of the German divisions.

INFANTRYMEN FIRING ON THE ENEMY during the house-to-house fighting in Saint-Malo (top). Infantrymen prepare to fire on enemy positions in Saint-Malo with their .30-caliber Browning machine gun M1917A1 (bottom). During the rapid advances to the east, the fighting on the Brittany Peninsula was still going on. On 17 August the last Germans in the citadel of Saint-Malo had been captured, and the U. S. division taking the city was moved to the southeast to cover the Loire flank west of Tours.

LE PETIT BEY                 LE GRAND BEY                 CITADEL

**THE HARBOR AT SAINT-MALO.** In the strongly defended forts in and around

FORT NATIONAL          FORT DU NAYE

the harbor stubborn groups of Germans held out against the U. S. attacking forces.

**SWABBING OUT THE BARREL OF AN 81-MM. MORTAR M1** before firing. During the battle of the Falaise–Argentan pocket U. S. artillery poured shells of all calibers into the pocket, and Allied aircraft hammered the Germans relentlessly.

PREPARING TO FIRE A 60-MM. MORTAR M2. The intense artillery fire and aerial bombing littered the countryside with all types of German vehicles and equipment. German commanders were able to control only small groups of their troops, so great was the confusion.

INFANTRYMEN, ARMED WITH CARBINES M1 AND RIFLE M1, discuss the action in which they have taken part (top). Engineers of an armored division relax in a French town during the advance of the U. S. troops (bottom). In the battle of the Falaise–Argentan pocket the Allies did not accomplish the utter destruction of the German forces in Normandy, but the enemy troops were broken as an effective fighting force and the way across France was open. During this period enemy losses included 70,000 killed and captured.

MEN AND VEHICLES ADVANCING TOWARD PARIS (3-inch gun motor carriage M10). Mopping-up the Falaise–Argentan pocket was assigned to troops of the 21 Army Group, while the First Army forces moved eastward. The Third Army was again moving eastward, and by the evening of 25 August the Allies held most of the Seine River west of Paris. On 15 August the Seventh U. S. Army invaded southern France and moved northward to join forces with the Allies in northern France.

240-MM. HOWITZER M1 FIRING on one of the Brittany fortresses (top). Cannoneers sight their 105-mm. howitzer M3, from a camouflaged position, during the seige of Brest (bottom). By 25 August only the three fortresses of Brest, Lorient, and Saint-Nazaire still offered resistance. A co-ordinated attack was launched on Brest by three infantry divisions supported by artillery of all calibers.

**INFANTRYMEN AND AID MEN ADVANCE ON BREST.** In this area the Germans blew up pillboxes to avoid their capture and some of the U. S. attackers were killed or wounded in the blasts.

A PORTION OF THE HARBOR AT BREST. This city on the Atlantic Ocean, with its good docks and harbors, was desirable as a supply port of entry. The enemy forces held out here until 18 September 1944, at which time the Allies had moved

so far to the east that the distance from Brest to the front lines was too great to make Brest an important landing point. Also the port was so badly damaged during the fighting that it became practically useless.

MEMBERS OF THE FRENCH RESISTANCE FIGHTING in the streets of Paris. The Allies had originally intended to bypass Paris so as to avoid its destruction in an assault. On 19 August 1944 fighting between the Germans and the French Forces of the Interior broke out in the city. The French were soon in need of relief, because of the shortage of ammunition, and Allied forces were shifted to take the city. Meeting with little resistance, a French armored division and a U. S. infantry division entered the city and by noon on 25 August the German commander formally surrendered.

PARISIANS SCATTER as a German sniper fires at them during the celebration of the Allied entry into Paris (top). U. S. troops march down the Champs Elysées during a victory parade in Paris (bottom). The last German resistance ceased in Paris on 27 August, and the next day the city was turned over to a French general who was to be the military governor.

AN 8-INCH GUN M1 BEING TOWED INTO POSITION by a high-speed 18-ton
M4 tractor (top). The crew of an 8-inch howitzer fires on the enemy across the Seine
River (bottom). The Canadian First Army cleaned up the enemy pockets west of the
Seine by 31 August, and the U. S. forces regrouped to pursue the enemy east of the
river and begin their drive toward Germany.

TOWED 155-MM. GUNS M1 CROSS A BAILEY BRIDGE over the Seine. U. S. troops advanced northeast from the Seine River bridgeheads to take Reims and Châlons-sur-Marne.

3-INCH GUN AND .50-CALIBER MACHINE GUN of an M10 tank destroyer fire on enemy troops trying to destroy a Marne River bridge. On 26 August Château-Thierry was captured. On 28 August Châlons-sur-Marne was taken and the following day Reims fell.

AN M4A1 TANK passes a burning German vehicle. By 30 August Saint-Dizier was reached and on 31 August the ground east of the Meuse River near Commercy was seized while Verdun was captured and the Meuse River crossed in that area. At the end of August the drives of the First and Third U. S. Armies were slowed down by lack of fuel.

ENGINEERS LAYING A GASOLINE PIPELINE in France. In an effort to transport fuel to the front-line units of the Allies, three fuel pipelines were laid across France. This also relieved the road traffic which became more and more congested as the number of Allied troops in France increased.

MEDICAL AID MEN MOVE UP UNDER FIRE to give first aid to a wounded infantryman (top). A wounded German is given medical aid by U. S. soldiers (bottom). By 3 September First Army troops had cleared most of the army's zone south of the Belgian border. On that day the remnants of twenty disorganized divisions were trapped before they could reach the Belgian border and 25,000 men were quickly liquidated. The British entered Brussels on 3 September and were also closing in on Le Havre, one of the major port cities on the coast.

**A LIGHT ARMORED CAR M8 ENTERING BELGIUM.** On 1 September 1944, Supreme Headquarters, Allied Expeditionary Force (SHAEF), was established at Versailles and assumed the active direction of the 12th and 21 Army Groups. During this period the main problem was that of supplying the racing armored columns since the only points of entry were the beaches and Cherbourg, a distance too far removed from the Allied forces advancing to the German frontier. By early September supply trucks were traveling 600 to 900 miles in round trips to carry fuel, ammunition, and rations to the combat units.

75-MM. HOWITZER MOTOR CARRIAGES M8 in Belgium (top). 155-mm. gun motor carriage M12 firing in Belgium (bottom). In spite of the shortage of supplies the pursuit of the enemy continued between 4 and 14 September 1944, with the greatest Allied gains being made on the northern front. On 4 September the British forces captured the port city of Antwerp, one of the greatest prizes of the war. On 12 September the city of Le Havre surrendered. These two cities were of extreme importance because of their port facilities and their nearness to the battle front.  In both harbors the enemy had carried out measures to render the ports useless, but they were not too badly damaged to prevent repair.

LIGHT ARMORED CAR M8 of a reconnaissance unit stops during its drive through Belgium toward the border of the Netherlands (top). Advancing infantrymen ride on a 3-inch gun motor carriage M10 (bottom). By 14 September 1944 the sustained drive of the First Army had stopped and the Germans were fighting on their own soil for the first time in many years.

INFANTRYMEN MOVING AN ASSAULT BOAT down to the banks of the Moselle River at Dornot (top); crossing the Moselle (bottom). Efforts to obtain enough gasoline were generally unavailing and most of the units of the Third Army were halted at the Moselle. On 5 September a crossing was made north of Nancy while on 8 September another was made below Metz. The Germans made numerous counterattacks and occupied the forts around Metz, determined to hold the line in this area.

BOEING B–17 FLYING THROUGH HEAVY FLAK over Germany en route to
a target (top). The Heinkel aircraft factory during an air attack (bottom).

MARTIN B-26'S RETURNING FROM A MISSION along the German border in support of the Third Army's ground attack. The medium bomber in the upper foreground of the above picture had operated in the ETO for some time, as is shown by the dark-painted fuselage. The plane in the lower foreground has an unpainted fuselage which enabled it to attain higher speeds.

INFANTRYMEN CROSS THE MOSELLE as a ¼-ton truck carries wounded men
to the rear (top). M4A1 medium tank fording a canal (bottom). On 10 September
an attack was launched to secure bridgeheads over the Moselle below Epinal, which
was reached on 14 September. The city of Nancy fell on 15 September.

INFANTRYMEN ADVANCING in the outskirts of Brest. While the Third Army was battling a determined enemy on the Moselle, U. S. forces were still trying to reduce the fortress of Brest. On 5 September the Ninth U. S. Army became operational in France and assumed the task of eliminating the remaining fortresses on the Brittany Peninsula.

AN 8-INCH GUN M1 FIRING ON GERMAN INSTALLATIONS in Brest. Artillery units attacking Brest were reinforced, mostly with medium and heavy caliber guns and, after sufficient ammunition had been accumulated, a strong attack was launched on 8 September by three infantry divisions.

90-MM. GUN MOTOR CARRIAGE M36 firing at an enemy pillbox in Brest (top). 76-mm. gun motor carriage M18 guarding a street intersection in Brest (bottom). On 14 September the fortress of Brest was still for the most part in German hands, despite all efforts to reduce the strongly fortified positions.

NEWLY CONSTRUCTED TREADWAY PONTON BRIDGE over the Moselle
River.

# RHINELAND CAMPAIGN
15 September 1944–15 December 1944

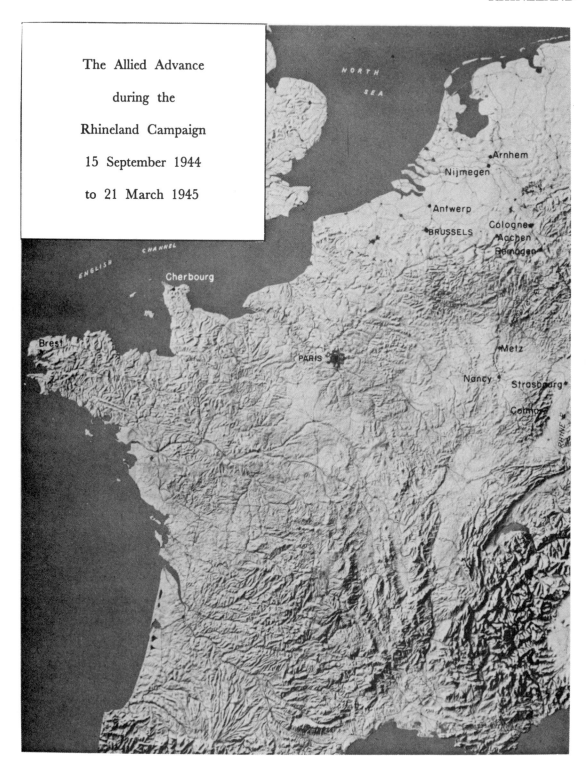

The Allied Advance
during the
Rhineland Campaign
15 September 1944
to 21 March 1945

SECTION IV

# Rhineland Campaign
# 15 September–15 December 1944*

On 15 September 1944 the Allied forces that had invaded southern France came under control of the Supreme Commander, Allied Expeditionary Force. This added the 6th Army Group to the forces opposing the enemy along the German frontier, making a total of forty-eight Allied divisions in the European Theater of Operations. In a little over three months, 6 June–15 September 1944, the Western Allies had carried their offensives from the Normandy beaches to the western borders of Germany. During the next three months little, if any, progress was made. Several factors contributed to this general slow-down. As fall and winter approached, rain, mud, and snow greatly hindered operations and made living conditions extremely trying. The terrain became more difficult since many rivers and streams had to be crossed and rough, wooded, and hilly country was encountered. Enemy resistance stiffened as the Allies reached the German border. But more important than any other single factor was the problem of supplying the large forces which had advanced so rapidly that they had outrun their supplies.

During this period, as the Allies came to the West Wall and the Rhine, severe fighting took place all along the front. Some of the most difficult operations of the war in western Europe occurred during the Rhineland Campaign as battles were fought in the Arnhem area, the Schelde estuary, the Huertgen Forest, the Aachen sector, the Metz and Saar regions, and the Belfort and Saverne Gaps. On 15 December the efforts of the Allies in the Rhineland were interrupted when the enemy broke through the lines in the Ardennes, causing a shift of troops to the Ardennes to reinforce the lines there.

---

*See H. M. Cole, *The Lorraine Campaign,* Washington, D. C., 1950; and Gordon A. Harrison and Forest C. Pogue, Jr., The Rhineland and Central Germany, now in preparation for the series U. S. ARMY IN WORLD WAR II.

ENLISTED MAN WALKING THROUGH MUD in his bivouac area. The Allied advance was halted at the German border by poor weather conditions, difficult terrain, stiffening German resistance, and, most of all, by lack of supplies. At this time the decision was made to employ the greatest strength in the north to attain flanking bridgeheads across the lower Rhine River beyond the main fortifications of the West Wall. This area was chosen for the drive since the terrain to the south was considered unsuitable for a rapid advance because of the mountainous and forested country.

PLANES TOWING GLIDERS take off for the invasion of the Netherlands, 17 September 1944. The First Allied Airborne Army launched its attack to secure a bridgehead across the Rhine in the Arnhem area. Complete surprise was achieved and the drops and glider landings were effective and in most cases were made in the prescribed areas. During the following ten days the fighting was severe with repeated German counterattacks. However, the railroad bridge across the Waal River in the Nijmegen area was captured on 20 September and remained in Allied hands. By the end of September the corridor was widened somewhat and the operation was considered a success even though the Allies were forced to evacuate most of the attacking troops after numerous casualties were suffered.

PARATROOPERS ADVANCING UNDER ENEMY FIRE in the Arnhem area (top). A captured German self-propelled assault gun (*Sturmgeschuetz* 7.5-cm. *Stu. K. 40*) (bottom). During the entire operation in the Netherlands which lasted for thirty days, from 17 September to 16 October 1944, over 5,500 planes and 2,500 gliders transported 34,000 men, and over 1,900 vehicles, 500 artillery pieces, and 5,000 tons of supplies. The airborne army suffered more than 13,000 casualties in killed, wounded, or missing.

INFANTRYMEN FOLLOWING A TANK during the advance north of Aachen (top). Infantrymen riding on an M4 medium tank-dozer through the West Wall, while others follow on foot (bottom). The last two weeks in September were spent by the First Army in probing the enemy's defenses along the frontier. On 2 October an attack was launched across the German border about eight miles north of Aachen. Progress during the next two weeks was slow as troops fought their way through six miles of West Wall, or "Siegfried Line," fortifications.

A 57-MM. ANTITANK GUN M1 being unlimbered from a half-track during the street fighting in Aachen (top). A Browning .30-caliber machine gun M1919A4 being fired at the enemy in Aachen (bottom). The German troops in Aachen refused a surrender ultimatum on 11 October 1944, and during the next three days the city was subjected to intense aerial bombardment and artillery fire. Infantrymen entered the city on 13 October and after fierce house-to-house fighting almost completely occupied Aachen by 20 October. The following day the garrison surrendered, making Aachen the first German city to fall to the Allies. The First U. S. Army then began preparations for a drive to the Rhine as soon as supplies and reinforcements should become available.

WEST RAILROAD YARDS

A PORTION OF THE CITY OF AACHEN. During the bitter fighting the Allies found it necessary to use all types of artillery weapons, from the 155-mm. gun to the

LOUSBERG

smaller guns of tank destroyers, at point blank range to reduce the heavily fortified
buildings occupied by enemy troops.

BRIDGEHEAD ACROSS THE MOSELLE south of Metz near Arnaville. While
the U. S. First Army was driving toward the Rhine in the vicinity of Bonn and
Cologne, the Third Army was holding its positions pending the improvement of the
supply situation. The Ninth Army moved up from Brittany and took its position
between the First and Third Armies in the Ardennes sector. The battle of Brest ended
on 18 September 1944, and except for enemy resistance in the Atlantic coast port
cities of Lorient and Saint-Nazaire, the Brittany Peninsula was completely in Allied
hands.

M4 MEDIUM TANKS on a street in Lunéville (top). U. S. troops firing a captured German 88-mm. gun in the vicinity of Metz (bottom). The period from 25 September to 7 November 1944 was the most unproductive phase of the U. S. Third Army's operations on the Continent. Troops closed in on the Moselle north of Thionville and consolidated their positions east of Nancy. On 18 September the Germans launched a counterattack near Lunéville but were stopped in their tracks. Two other attacks on 22 and 24 September were also stopped and the Germans began to retreat on the night of 1–2 October.

FIVE-GALLON WATER CANS loaded in a quarter-ton trailer being filled at an
Engineer water point. The Engineers were responsible for the purification of drinking
water and set up water points from which all units located in the area drew their
daily supply.

BREAD BEING PLACED ON COOLING RACKS in a Quartermaster bakery
after being removed from the ovens.

INFANTRYMEN FIRING a .30-caliber Browning machine gun M1917A1 on the outskirts of Metz (top). Infantry patrol entering Metz (bottom). For two months the U. S. Third Army was stalled in the vicinity of Metz, the fortress which would have to be captured before any substantial advance eastward could be made. Metz dominated three invasion routes into Germany from France: the valley of the Moselle through Trier and Coblenz; the Kaiserslautern Pass through Saarbruecken to Mainz and Worms; and the route through the Saverne Gap from Sarrebourg to Strasbourg and the Rhine. Only once in modern times had the fortress of Metz fallen to an attacking army—in 1871 the defending French troops surrendered to the Prussians.

90-MM. GUN MOTOR CARRIAGE M36 in Metz. The capture of Metz was hindered by rain and floods which canceled the heavy air support and made the advance difficult for the ground forces. The attack started on 8 November with only artillery support and it was not until 22 November that the city was finally clear of all enemy pockets of resistance. The last of the forts which ringed the city was taken on 13 December. The Third Army was then confronted by one of the strongest sections of the West Wall, and since its reduction would require a vast amount of artillery support, the attacks were suspended until the necessary ammunition could be brought up.

MOSELLE RIVER
        CANAL           FORT ST. JULIEN

THE CITY OF METZ showing the location of two of the forts which ringed the city.

These and other forts presented problems to the assaulting troops.

**THANKSGIVING DINNER AT THE FRONT.** During October and November 1944 the cold, rain, fog, and floods made living conditions of the front-line troops miserable. The battle against the weather was as difficult as that against the enemy.

ENGINEERS HAULING BRIDGING EQUIPMENT in flooded areas of the
Moselle River. The flooded rivers and smaller streams made the task of bridging
extremely difficult during this period of the fighting along the German frontier since,
in addition to the wider than normal spans necessary to cross the rivers, the weather
was cold and rainy, adding to the hardships of those employed in the task.

TRACK EXTENSIONS being put on the track of a medium tank. The maneuverability of tanks and other tracked vehicles was greatly hampered by mud along the front lines. Confronted by a problem more serious than anticipated, Ordnance personnel quickly designed and started production of track extensions at the rate of 156 separate pieces for each tank. Civilian manufacturing facilities were utilized in France and Belgium and before the program was completed 1,500,000 extensions had been made and welded to the tank tracks.

AN M4A3 MEDIUM TANK fitted with track extensions maneuvering through soupy ground. Track extensions were so devised as to give better flotation and traction through the November mud.

105-MM. HOWITZER M3 shelling enemy positions. After the capture of Aachen the First and Ninth Armies prepared for a new offensive. The initial objectives were to capture bridgeheads over the Roer River in the vicinity of Dueren and make advances toward Juelich. At the same time the defensive positions in the Ardennes area were held. After a four-day delay the weather cleared and planes of the Allied air forces began the attack. Several towns including Dueren and Juelich were reduced to rubble.

MEDIUM TANKS FIRING during the assault toward the Roer River (top). 155-mm. gun motor carriage M12 firing on enemy held positions (bottom). In spite of the elaborate preparations made for the attack and the great concentration of combat power, progress was extremely slow. Each of the towns was woven into a network in which each house had to be reduced, and each foot of the muddy ground was defended to the last by the enemy troops. The attack plowed on determinedly in the mud and cold and on 3 December 1944 the Ninth Army came to the Roer. The First Army also attacked until the river was reached. (Note the newer type track with cleats on the treads to give better traction.)

3-INCH GUN MOTOR CARRIAGES M10 move up in the Huertgen Forest area.
Troops of the First and Ninth Armies had been fighting their way toward Schmidt
since September in one of the most bitterly contested actions of the war. One of the
major obstacles in the advance was the Huertgen Forest which covered roughly the
triangle of Aachen–Dueren–Monschau. In the vicinity of Schmidt were dams which
controlled the level of the Roer River, and while these were still in enemy hands
water could be released flooding the valley of the Roer. It was therefore considered
necessary to take this area and the dams before the river was crossed by the attacking
U. S. forces.

INFANTRYMEN pushing through the Huertgen Forest near Vossenack, Germany (top). Vehicles moving up a muddy road through the forest (bottom). The Germans had strengthened this natural barrier by the clever use of wire, pillboxes, and mines, and the U. S. infantrymen, restricted by the rough wooded terrain, were forced to fight for the most part without the aid of artillery or air support. On 13 December the attack on the dams was renewed but the going was still slow. Casualties to the two armies advancing in this area were high.

KALL RIVER          OUTSKIRTS OF VOSSENACK

KOMMERSCHEIDT AND THE SURROUNDING AREA. The terrain of the Schmidt and Vossenack areas, like that of the Huertgen Forest, was hilly and wooded.

KALL RIVER

The Roer River dams in this area were important objectives for the Allies during this part of the campaign.

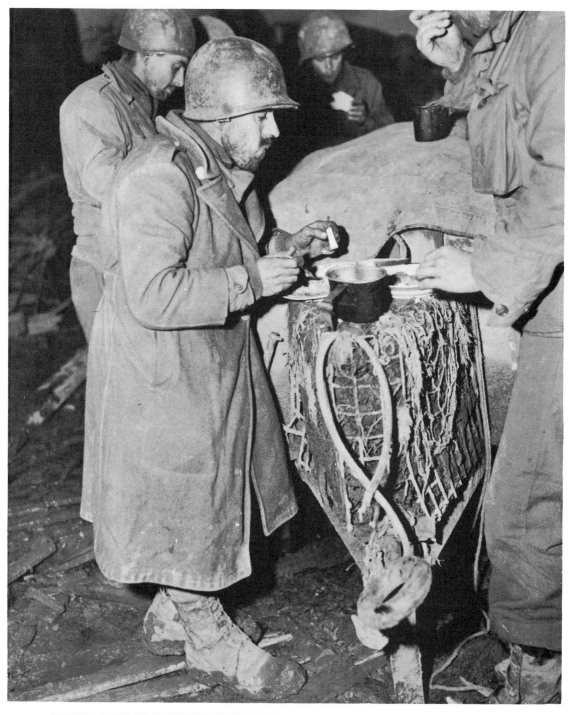

TIRED, DIRTY, HUNGRY INFANTRYMEN eat their first hot meal after fifteen days of siege of the town of Huertgen.

BATTLE-WEARY GERMANS who were among the last to surrender after the battle of the Huertgen Forest which lasted for several weeks.

MINE EXPLODER T1E3 attached to a medium tank. This model was an improvement over the earlier one because of its chain-driven exploder disks. On the first models the exploder disks rolled freely and were not power driven. The new model also had a higher degree of indestructibility and greater maneuverability and could be driven in mud eighteen inches deep and across broken terrain. The T1E3 could be driven across a Class 70 military bridge.

FIRING ROCKETS during the fighting in the Huertgen Forest area. In the above pictures 4.5-inch multiple rocket launchers T27 are mounted on 2½-ton trucks and consist of eight tubes in a single bank. Two banks are mounted on each of the trucks with the rockets being fired at half-second intervals.

FOG OIL being used to produce a smoke screen to limit observation during river crossings. This function of the Chemical Warfare companies was utilized in covering the activities of troops at ports, airfields, docks, and harbors in addition to concealing vital points from direct enemy air observation during advances and river crossings. When the danger of aerial attack was practically eliminated it was still used against ground observation. By means of a generator the fog oil was converted into a white fog which was used effectively whenever the wind conditions were not strong enough to disperse the screen too rapidly.

90-MM. ANTIAIRCRAFT GUN M1 being fired at a German flying bomb passing over Belgium. Liège was subjected to an attack by these robot bombs and suffered considerable damage. Because of the great speed of these weapons it was difficult to combat them, but later with the utilization of the newly developed proximity fuse, the seriousness of the threat of the flying bombs diminished.

SEVENTH ARMY VEHICLES CROSSING THE MOSELLE. During the later half of September the 6th Army Group's positions were consolidated, boundaries were adjusted, divisions were shifted into their proper zones, and plans were made for the advance to the Rhine.

4.2-INCH CHEMICAL MORTAR being fired during the advance of the Seventh
Army, October 1944.

THREE INFANTRYMEN of the Seventh Army looking down on a village in France from a hilltop which has been under heavy mortar and artillery fire.

INFANTRYMEN CLIMB UPON AN M5 LIGHT TANK in preparation for an advance. In November 1944 the Seventh Army was to make the main effort of the 6th Army Group in an advance toward Sarrebourg and Strasbourg. In the south the French First Army was to drive through the Belfort Gap.

ARTILLERY LIAISON PLANES grounded in the Seventh Army area. In the Vosges mountains snow drifted over the roads, the temperature dropped below freezing, and streams overflowed their banks.

**INFANTRYMEN OF THE SEVENTH ARMY** advance through snow and sleet. The attack of 6th Army Group was to breach the Vosges mountains whereupon the two armies would join in the Rhine plain to isolate the enemy's Vosges positions. Short of artillery ammunition, the troops slugged it out with the enemy over difficult terrain and in increasingly bad weather, with the infantry carrying most of the burden.

SEVENTH ARMY ARTILLERYMEN loading a 105-mm. howitzer M2A1. The attack was launched, after an all-night artillery preparation, in a snow storm on the morning of 13 November 1944. At noon on 14 November the French First Army jumped off in its attack. On 16 November the French broke through the Belfort defenses and on 20 November reached the Rhine. Mulhouse fell on 22 November despite a quickly established enemy defensive line.

A 105-MM. HOWITZER MOTOR CARRIAGE M7 being fired on German positions in the Rhine Valley (top). Infantrymen wait in a shallow zig-zag trench before advancing (bottom). On 20 November Sarrebourg was captured and on 22 November Saverne fell. By 27 November Strasbourg and its ring of defending forts had been taken. After the collapse of the enemy positions in the Vosges, the Seventh Army attacked northward and by the middle of December had crossed the German frontier on a 22-mile front and penetrated the West Wall defenses northeast of Wissembourg. In the meantime the German forces which had been driven from the Vosges maintained their bridgehead in the Colmar area, which became known as the Colmar pocket before it was finally liquidated.

REWARDS FOR STANDING IN LINE: men receiving typhus booster shots (top);
men exchanging their French and Belgium francs for German marks (bottom).

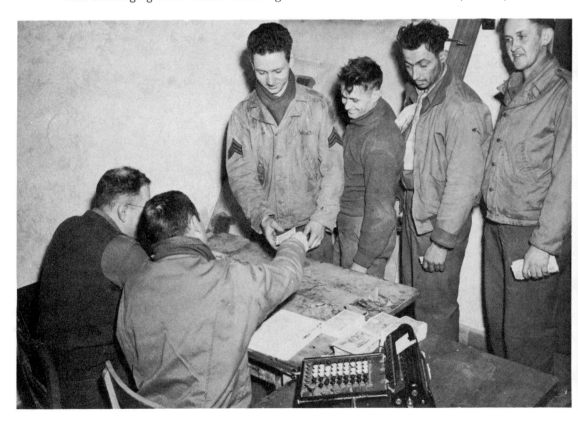

WOUNDED SOLDIERS BEING EVACUATED in tracked vehicles during the winter months. Cargo carrier M29 (top); half-track personnel carrier M3 (bottom).

OPENING THE VALVE ON A GASOLINE PIPELINE. The critical fuel situation of September, which had stalled the armored divisions at the West Wall, was materially improved by December. At that time three main pipelines were constructed or under construction: one for the northern armies, one for the central armies, and another for the southern armies.

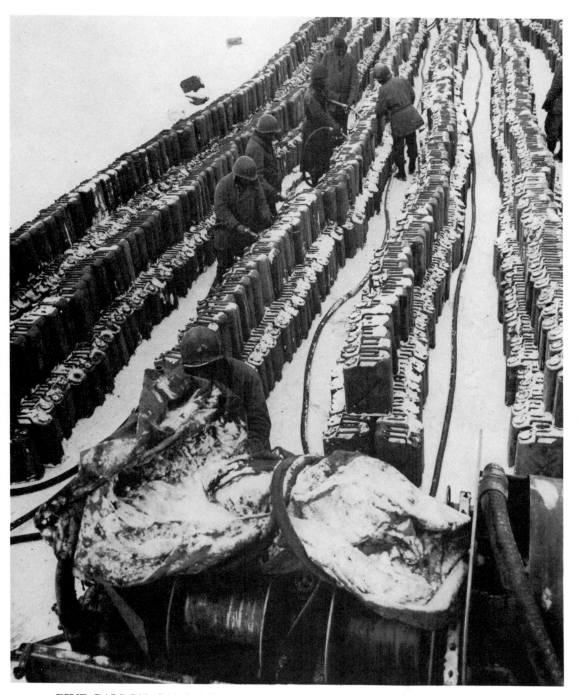

FIVE-GALLON CANS BEING FILLED WITH GASOLINE at a distribution point. On 15 December 1944 the armies had from a five- to nine-day supply of gasoline on hand while the Ninth Air Force had over 600,000 gallons of aviation gasoline and oil stored in the Namur area.

ARMY SUPPLIES BEING UNLOADED at Antwerp. The greatest single factor in the improved supply situation was the port of Antwerp which became operational on 27 November. Despite heavy attacks from the German "V" weapons the port discharged cargo which was badly needed by the forces fighting along the German frontier. Utah and Omaha Beaches ceased operations in November and then only the larger port cities were used as supply ports of entry.

AMPHIBIAN TRUCKS LOADING SUPPLIES into railroad cars after bringing them ashore from ships in the harbor of Le Havre (top). In addition to Antwerp, the major Allied ports were Le Havre, Ghent (opened in January 1945), Rouen, Cherbourg, and Marseille. An enlisted man reading a directive, signed by the theater commander, concerning the conservation of tires, an effort made to curtail the wasteful use of equipment and supplies (bottom). While in general the supply situation was much improved over that in September there were still critical shortages in a wide variety of items including antifreeze, tires, post exchange rations, miscellaneous signal equipment, and some winter clothing.

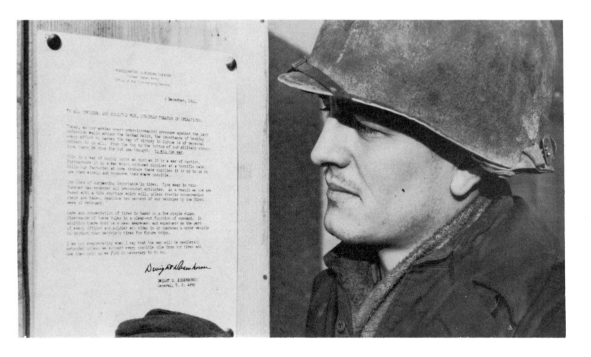

2½-TON TRUCKS PICK UP RATIONS at a Belgian railhead (top). 10-ton semitrailers loaded with rations at Antwerp, ready to be hauled to the forward depots (bottom). The multiple-drive motor transport vehicles were continuously on the move and made possible the supplying of troops during the rapid advances.

# ARDENNES-ALSACE CAMPAIGN

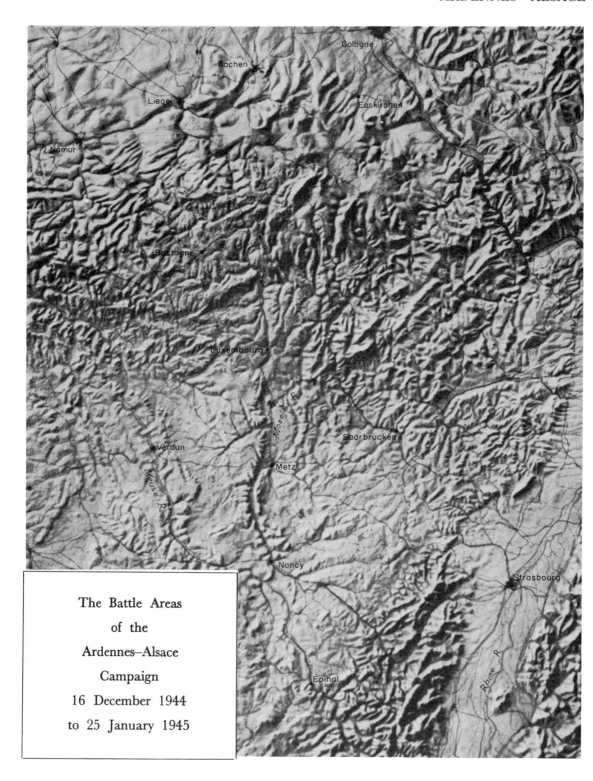

The Battle Areas
of the
Ardennes–Alsace
Campaign
16 December 1944
to 25 January 1945

## SECTION V

# Ardennes–Alsace Campaign*

In mid-December 1944 the Allies stopped along the German border, but continued to attack in the Saar and Roer regions, while they concentrated the majority of their strength for an attack in the north. The Germans, taking advantage of their continuous front along the West Wall, planned a counterattack to strike the Allies in one of the weakest portions of the line—the Ardennes sector. The ultimate goals of this German operation were to capture the port city of Antwerp, sever the major Allied supply lines emanating from that port, and destroy the Allied forces north of the Antwerp–Brussels–Bastogne line.

Early on the morning of 16 December the German armies struck the Allied troops located in Belgium and Luxembourg. The Allies holding this portion of the line were too thinly dispersed to offer any great resistance against the powerful enemy attack and were forced to fall back. While the defenders fought the Germans, Allied armies shifted their drives and troops were rushed to the Ardennes to reinforce the hard hit units along the front from Monschau to Echternach. After severe fighting during late December 1944 and early January 1945 the Germans were defeated and by 25 January the Allies were once more ready to move toward Germany through the West Wall defenses. During the Ardennes–Alsace Campaign winter set in and the cold weather and snow-covered terrain made operations and living conditions extremely difficult.

During this period the British forces in the north eliminated the Germans in the Roermond triangle and captured the enemy bridgehead west of the Roer River. The U. S. and French troops of the 6th Army Group fought a determined enemy in Lorraine and Alsace and by 25 January had driven the attacking Germans back across the Moder River.

---

*See Hugh M. Cole, The Ardennes, and James D. Hamilton, Southern France and Alsace, both volumes now in preparation for the series U. S. ARMY IN WORLD WAR II.

The Ardennes–Alsace Campaign, which delayed the Rhineland Campaign for six weeks, secured no major terrain objectives for either side. The Germans, who had employed some of their best remaining units, lost nearly 250,000 men, 600 tanks and assault guns, and about 1,600 airplanes. The Allies suffered 72,000 casualties.

On 6 January 1945 the Fifteenth U. S. Army became operational on the Continent and was assigned to the 12th Army Group, taking over many of that army group's responsibilities in the rear areas.

**GERMAN SOLDIER WITH AMMUNITION BELTS** moves forward during the enemy counterattack in the Ardennes. German morale was higher than at any time since the Allies had landed, partly because the individual soldier had been propagandized into believing that this was the opportunity to destroy the Allied troops in the west. At 0530 on 16 December 1944 three German armies attacked on a 50-mile front in eastern Belgium and northern Luxembourg. This battle was popularly known as the Battle of the Bulge.

ENEMY TROOPS PASS BURNING U. S. EQUIPMENT. The initial German attacks, following a heavy artillery preparation, were launched all along the front, roughly from Monschau to Echternach. The first objective was to secure the high ground of the Hohe Venn but the drive by the enemy met with stiff resistance and he was forced to commit his armor before noon on 16 December. Further attacks in the northern sector were no more successful and by night the Germans were still fighting at the approaches to the Elsenborn Ridge.

A GERMAN SOLDIER waving members of his unit forward. Spurred on by expressions of the German commanders such as "Forward to and over the Meuse" and "We gamble everything now—we cannot fail," enemy troops drove forward in a determined effort to defeat the Allies. South of the Elsenborn Ridge in the vicinity of the Losheim Gap U. S. troops were overwhelmed and forced to withdraw. By evening the enemy, though blocked in the north, had broken through the thinly held American line and drove toward Stavelot and Huy, the first objective on the Meuse River. Still further to the south in the Echternach area, the U. S. forces stopped the enemy after he had made limited gains. The Allied situation along the front was extremely grave.

TYPICAL ARDENNES TERRAIN. The rough, wooded tableland of the Ardennes in eastern Belgium and northern Luxembourg is broken by many small streams which become serious obstacles during periods of heavy rain or thaw. The Ardennes con-

tains a fair primary but poor secondary road system. Because of the rough terrain the main centers of the road net assumed great importance during the Battle of the Bulge. Heavy snow made infantry maneuver difficult and seriously limited tank movement.

GERMAN "KING TIGER" OR "TIGER ROYAL" heavy tank passing a line of captured U. S. soldiers being marched to the rear (top). U. S. prisoners of the enemy taken during the early fighting in the Battle of the Bulge (bottom). Two U. S. regiments near Saint-Vith were surrounded and most of the men were taken prisoner before U. S. reinforcements could arrive on the scene. The enemy attacks on Elsenborn Ridge were stopped by these U. S. reinforcements on 17 December, but this help came too late to save from capture the men shown above and those of an artillery battery who were caught by an enemy armored column south of Malmédy.

AN INFANTRYMAN PAUSING IN HIS ADVANCE through the forest. During the first ten days of the battle confusion reigned as hastily shifted troops arrived to reinforce the efforts of the isolated units attempting to halt the enemy attack.

A BATTERY OF 155-MM. HOWITZERS M1 being emplaced (top). Members of an airborne division moving up through the forest (bottom). On 18 December German patrols passed through a gap between Malmédy and Saint-Vith and continued as far west as Werbomont. Other enemy troops tried to push north through Stavelot but were stopped by a blown bridge over the Ambleve River and by an improvised task force consisting of U. S. infantrymen, engineers, and tank destroyers. Engineer demolitions and effective use for the first time of the new proximity fuze by artillery strengthened the north shoulder of the growing salient. During the first week of the Battle of the Bulge most planes were grounded because of extremely poor flying weather.

BATTLE-WEARY TROOPS being relieved of front-line duty as reinforcements arrive to take over (top). Infantrymen batter down the door of a house where German snipers are holding out in the town of Stavelot (bottom). On 19 December the north and south flanks continued to hold, and road centers of Saint-Vith and Bastogne were still occupied by U. S. troops though almost surrounded by the enemy. The enemy captured Stoumont but the U. S. forces strengthened the line between Malmédy and Stavelot and with additional reinforcements began to attack the enemy east of Stoumont. To the south the enemy took up blocking positions south of the Sauer River with some troops as far west as the Arlon–Bastogne highway.

CREW OF A MULTIPLE GUN MOTOR CARRIAGE M16 waiting to fire on
an enemy plane as vapor trails fill the sky. On 20 December control of the First and
Ninth U. S. Armies passed to the 21 Army Group, while the Third U. S. Army
and a corps of the First Army remained under 12th Army Group control. On 23
December the weather cleared sufficiently for planes of the Eighth and Ninth U. S.
Air Forces and the British Bomber Command to begin a large-scale aerial assault on
German positions and installations. The German planes which were sent up in greater
strength than at any other time since the invasion were no match for the Allies.
On Christmas Day the First U. S. Army launched an attack and made contact with
the British forces in the northern section of the front. For the first time since 16
December a continuous Allied front was established.

PART OF AN ARMORED DIVISION of the Third Army moving into the Ardennes. At the beginning of the Battle of the Bulge Third Army was regrouping for an attack on the West Wall in the Saar area. On 18 December an armored division was turned north toward the Ardennes sector and was followed by an infantry division the next day. The 6th Army Group was turned north to take over the area held by Third Army, which during a period of six days broke off its general attack in the Saar region, turned left, moved more than a 100 miles over unknown winter roads, and mounted an attack with six divisions.

C–47's CARRYING SUPPLIES to surrounded U. S. troops in Bastogne (top). Infantrymen in Bastogne (bottom). While Third Army was advancing to relieve the armored and airborne troops in Bastogne, the battle for the city was being waged. The enemy surrounding the city numbered 45,000 while within Bastogne there were about 18,000 U. S. troops. The commander of the troops in the city refused to surrender to the Germans and continued to hold out against all attacks. The defenders, cut off from their sources, were supplied by airdrops during this period. On 24 December over 100 tons of supplies were dropped.

INFANTRYMEN FIRE AT GERMAN TROOPS in the advance to relieve the surrounded paratroopers in Bastogne. In foreground a platoon leader indicates the target to a rifleman by actually firing on the target. In Bastogne the defenders were badly in need of relief, they were attacked nightly by German aircraft, supplies were critically low in spite of the airdrops, and the wounded could not be given proper attention because of the shortage of medical supplies. After an advance which had been slow, U. S. relief troops entered Bastogne at 1645 on 26 December 1944.

INFANTRYMEN ADVANCE ON BASTOGNE (top). Prisoners taken during the advance on Bastogne being evacuated (bottom). With the arrival of U. S. relief troops were forty truckloads of supplies which were delivered during the night of 26 December. 652 wounded men were evacuated from the area and the battle continued since the enemy had shifted a large portion of his attacking troops in this area. On the night of 26 December when the German advance was halted the Third Army, consisting of eight divisions and parts of two other battered divisions, faced elements of eleven German divisions between the Meuse and the Moselle.

105-MM. HOWITZER MOTOR CARRIAGE M7 of an armored unit on the alert near Bastogne. By 27 December more than thirty-five corps artillery battalions were firing approximately 19,000 rounds of ammunition daily in support of the Third Army. By the end of the year that army was supported by over 1,000 guns of 105-mm. caliber or larger. Christmas night the Third Army's artillery began using the new proximity fuze, which proved particularly effective in interdicting road junctions and harassing enemy positions.

ENGINEERS UNLOADING BARBED WIRE which was used in defensive measures against counterattacks.

ENGINEER PLANTING AN ANTITANK MINE on the shoulder of a road as a defensive measure during the fighting in the Ardennes.

BASTOGNE AND THE SURROUNDING AREA. Although the corridor which had been opened to Bastogne remained in U. S. hands it was far from secure as it was less than 300 yards wide in some places. The Germans were passing to the defensive in other sectors and concentrating on their attacks in the Bastogne area.

BASTOGNE CREEK          RAILROAD

The mission of the Third Army was to widen the corridor, push attacks on Saint-Vith, and at the same time reinforce its attacking units. During this period of the fighting in Europe adverse weather conditions added greatly to the problems, and the snow- and sleet-covered roads hampered the movement of troops.

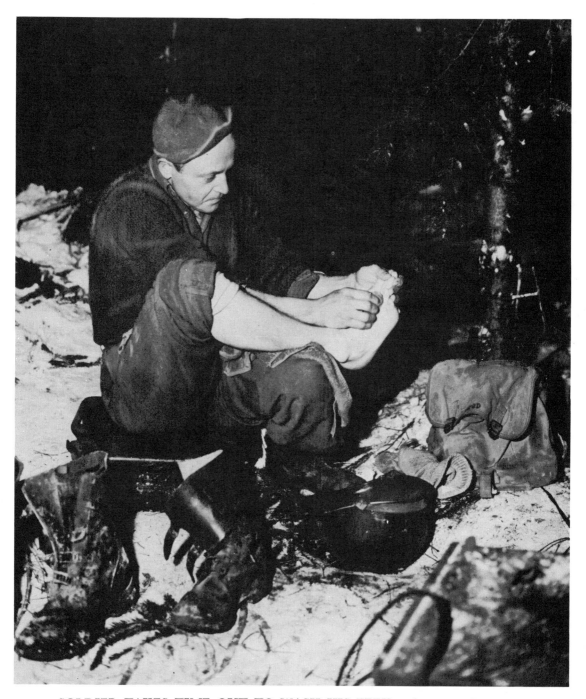

SOLDIER TAKES TIME OUT TO WASH HIS FEET and put on dry socks.
The cold weather combined with the snow and dampness caused many cases of
trench foot during this period. It was difficult when wearing the regular leather shoes
to keep one's feet dry and warm, but frequent washing and changing of socks helped.

AN ENLISTED MAN PUTS ON A NEW PAIR OF SHOEPACS. The shoepac, which was supplied to as many of the troops as possible at this time, helped to overcome the heavy incidence of trench foot among the U. S. troops fighting in cold and extremely wet climates. This shoe was rubber-bottomed with a leather top and was worn with a heavy ski sock and felt innersole.

INFANTRYMEN WEARING SNOW CAPES over their normal clothing. Snow caught the U. S. troops without adequate camouflage, and strenuous efforts were made to improvise white suits out of mattress covers and linen collected from the civilians.

CAMOUFLAGED LIGHT ARMORED CAR M8 and one that has not been painted white, showing the effectiveness of snow camouflaging (top). A crew member of a 90-mm. gun motor carriage M36 throwing paint on the bogie wheels after painting the vehicle (bottom). Tanks, vehicles, and guns were camouflaged with white paint.

KNOCKED-OUT U. S. MEDIUM TANKS. During the last few days of December 1944 the main effort in Third Army zone was concentrated in the vicinity of Bastogne, while the situation in the rest of the army area remained static. Armored and infantry attacks achieved small gains during which many German counterattacks were made. Echternach was re-entered on 29 December and all enemy forces south of the Sauer River were cleared. The armored divisions continued to advance. One, in repulsing several counterattacks, suffered heavy casualties. On 3 January 1945 the last German attack was made on Bastone. It was unsuccessful.

MEN OF AN INFANTRY DIVISION climbing into box cars to move from the Brittany Peninsula to the U. S. Third Army zone. On 9 January 1945 a new attack was started after fresh troops had been brought into the battle area. The Germans offered fierce resistance in order to keep open their escape route to the east. On 16 January elements of an armored division of Third Army contacted those from First Army, closing the German salient just one month after the enemy had launched his counteroffensive in the Ardennes.

INFANTRYMEN BIVOUACKING IN THE WOODS (top) ; field mess (bottom).
Living conditions during the best of times were not too pleasant for the combat
soldier, but during the winter the hardships were greatly increased.

U. S. LIGHT TANKS which were captured by the enemy during the Battle of the
Bulge. Some of the more serious U. S. losses during this period were 1,284 machine
guns, 542 mortars, 1,344 jeeps, and 237 tanks. Not all of these losses were the result
of units being overrun—there was some evidence of unnecessary abandonment of
equipment, particularly among inexperienced troops.

MEMBERS OF AN ARMORED UNIT STAND GUARD beside their dug-in medium tank near Manhay, Belgium. From 27 December 1944 to 2 January 1945 the First U. S. Army was reorganizing and preparing to attack the Hotton–Houffalize axis. Heavy fighting continued all along the First Army front and by 30 December the important traffic centers of Marche, Hotton, and Manhay were secured.

AIRBORNE INFANTRYMEN on the alert man their .30-caliber machine gun (top). A member of a cavalry reconnaissance squadron checks his .30-caliber machine gun (bottom).

AIRBORNE TROOPS LOADING A SHELL into a 75-mm. pack howitzer M8. Between 16 December and 27 December First Army artillery units fired more ammunition than at any other time during the war except during the Normandy Campaign. An average of 800 weapons fired over 750,000 shells.

LOADING A 105-MM. SHELL into the howitzer of a Priest (top); snow on the camouflage net over a 155-mm. howitzer M1 helps conceal its position (bottom).

AN ARTILLERY PLANE with newly attached skis taking off (top); observation planes grounded during the bad weather (bottom).

MEN STRINGING BARBED WIRE DURING A BLIZZARD (top); tank crews keeping warm as they eat their rations (bottom).

MANHAY, BELGIUM. On 3 January 1945 an attack was launched west of Manhay in the First Army zone. Visibility was reduced to 200 yards and the temperature was near zero. The few roads were coated with ice and the snow off the roads was waist deep making it extremely difficult to maneuver. During the first day advances of almost 4,000 yards were made before a heavy snowfall halted the assault. On 5

January the attack was resumed and the La Roche–Vielsalm road was cut. La Roche was captured by the British on 10 January. The British troops were then withdrawn to regroup for the Rhineland Campaign. The Germans began to withdraw from the tip of the salient after becoming convinced that they had lost in their attempt to halt the Allies.

ELEMENTS OF THE FIRST AND THIRD ARMIES made contact at Houffalize on 16 January. While the U. S. units were still understrength, replacements to the theater had increased. Despite heavy fighting and poor living conditions, morale was high.

155-MM. GUN M1A1, with its barrel camouflaged by white cloth, firing in the Ardennes. The junction of First and Third Armies at Houffalize marked the achievement of tactical victory in the Ardennes. On 17 January the First Army reverted to 12th Army Group, but the Ninth U. S. Army remained under 21 Army Group. With the enemy withdrawing from the Ardennes the Allies resumed their advance toward the Rhine.

TWO GERMAN PRISONERS BEING BROUGHT IN (top). Papers of a U. S. vehicle driver being checked by a guard at a road intersection (bottom). During the fighting in the Ardennes some German paratroopers were dropped behind the U. S. lines. Others dressed in U. S. uniforms and driving U. S. vehicles were operating behind the American lines.

"KING TIGER" OR "ROYAL TIGER" (*Pz. Kpfw. VI (B) "Tiger"* with 8.8-cm. *Kw. K. 43*) (top). This tank, weighing 75 tons and designed for defensive warfare or for penetrating strong lines of defense, made its appearance in combat in 1944. It had heavy frontal armor and an 88-mm. gun which could traverse 360 degrees. Germany heavy tank, the Panther (*Pz. Kpfw.* with 7.5-cm. *Kw. K. 42–L/70*) (bottom). This tank, introduced in 1942, weighed 47 tons and had sloping frontal armor and a 75-mm. high-velocity gun.

BARBED WIRE BEING STRUNG as a defensive measure in the event of another enemy counterattack. In mid-January the enemy was still able to maintain a cohesive line, but the critical situation on the Russian front made necessary the shifting of troops to the eastern front while withdrawing to the security of the West Wall all committed troops facing the western Allies.

A SIGNAL CORPS LINEMAN repairing damaged telephone lines.

A TRUCK-MOUNTED CRANE swinging the barrel of an 8-inch gun from its transport wagon (top), and placing it on its carriage (bottom). The gun and cradle were transported on one vehicle and the carriage on another.

A CAMOUFLAGED 8-INCH GUN M1 located in the southern portion of the Third
Army zone. This gun was capable of firing a 240-pound projectile a distance of 20
miles. The troops left in this area were placed on the defensive during the fighting in
the Ardennes sector. Heavy artillery in the area fired on enemy installations in the
triangle of the Moselle and Saar Rivers and West Wall fortifications.

**A MEMBER OF A GLIDER REGIMENT,** armed with a rifle and a rocket launcher, returning from a three-hour tour of guard duty.

A TANKER SEWS HIS CLOTHING on an old sewing machine in front of his M4A3 medium tank.

SUPPLIES MOVING THROUGH BASTOGNE, 22 January 1945, on their way to the front-line troops. By the first of the year matériel losses in the Battle of the Bulge had been replaced and the combat units were again prepared to move forward.

MEDICAL AID MEN dragging a boatload of medical supplies down a snow and ice covered road to the banks of a stream they are to cross. From 17 to 24 January the Third Army continued to attack through Houffalize and reached the northern tip of Luxembourg on 24 January. In an advance to the east bridgeheads north of Clervaux on the Clerf River were secured on 23 January. During this period most of the area between the Sauer and the Our Rivers was cleared of enemy resistance. In a hurried effort to withdraw as many vehicles as possible the enemy lost over 1,700 vehicles to planes of the U. S. XIX Tactical Air Command.

A MEMBER OF AN 81-MM. MORTAR CREW listening to firing orders from a battalion command post.

INFANTRYMEN ADVANCING UNDER ENEMY SHELL FIRE. On 15 January 1945, on the left of the First Army zone, an attack was begun from the Butgenbach–Malmédy positions. By 19 January First Army had secured the defiles southwest of Butgenbach. The attack launched toward Saint-Vith continued to gain ground, and on 23 January Saint-Vith was recaptured.

FIRST ARMY TROOPS, wearing snow camouflage capes, advance.

MEN OF AN AIRBORNE UNIT preparing to board trucks which will take them
to a rest area after being relieved at the front. On 24 January the First and Third
Armies' boundary was shifted north in the general line Saint-Vith–Losheim–Ahr
River and attacks were to be renewed on the Saint-Vith–Bonn axis. First Army was
to breach the West Wall and secure the high ground in the vicinity of Blankenheim,
while Third Army was to attack with its left wing to cover the First Army.

AN M5 LIGHT TANK guarding a road in the U. S. Ninth Army area, 22 January. With the collapse of the German salient in the Ardennes, preparations were made for the offensive to the Rhine by 21 Army Group. The Germans held the triangle south of Roermond between the Meuse and Roer Rivers. This was a serious threat to the left flank of the Ninth Army and had to be eliminated before the army could advance across the Roer to the Rhine plain. The task of eliminating this salient was assigned to the British Second Army and by 26 January was completed.

SEVENTH ARMY TROOPS entering a fortress of the Maginot Line, near Bitche, France, which had been taken in the December fighting. Reduction of the strongly defended forts of the Maginot Line was halted when the Arsennes fighting began. The new Seventh Army front included the three following areas: the Saare Valley in Lorraine; the low Vosges mountains; and the northern Alsace plain between the mountains and the Rhine.

MEMBERS OF A SEVENTH ARMY ARTILLERY UNIT unloading powder charges for their 240-mm. howitzer (top); 3-inch gun motor carriage firing on enemy positions at night (bottom). On 20 December 1944 the 6th Army Group abandoned its offensive and relieved the Third Army in the region westward to Saarlautern to defend against any enemy penetration in Alsace–Lorraine. The offensive was stopped even though many pillboxes in the West Wall had been taken, and during the last ten days of December the Seventh Army regrouped its forces and deployed its troops.

CONVOY MOVING UP in the Seventh Army area during the fighting in Alsace (top); vehicles moving over snow-covered roads through the Vosges mountains (bottom).

BITCHE, FRANCE. The Seventh Army prepared an alternate main line of resistance along the old Maginot Line (Sarreguemines–Bitche–Lembach–Hatten–Sessen-
heim) and a final defensive position along the eastern slope of the Vosges. On 1
January 1945 the Germans attacked in the area between Sarre and Rohrbach and
drove ten miles into the U. S. lines, where the apppearance of powerful armored

reserves of the U. S. forces and Allied counterattacks caused the enemy to curtail its operation. Another New Year's Day attack by the Germans in the Bitche area was a more serious threat. After stubborn fighting on the part of the Allied troops the attack spent itself on 7 January. In the Bitche salient the fighting continued until 20 January before becoming stabilized.

TANKS OF AN ARMORED UNIT moving along a slippery road during a heavy snowstorm. In other 6th Army Group areas there was action along the front. As U. S. troops withdrew to the Maginot Line so that French troops could take over this portion of the front, the Germans followed closely. French troops in the Strasbourg area contained an enemy attack from the Colmar pocket. There was heavy activity in the U. S. zone near Hatten where the enemy, after suffering heavy losses, failed to break through the U. S. troops.

CAMOUFLAGED TANKS and infantrymen, wearing snow camouflage capes, moving over a snow-covered field. Toward the end of January a heavy snowfall slowed operations and on 25 January the enemy struck his final blow near Haguenau, France. On 26 January the Germans were driven back across the Moder River.

MEMBERS OF A CANNON COMPANY near Haguenau keep warm as best they can.

# RHINELAND CAMPAIGN
## 26 January 1945–21 March 1945

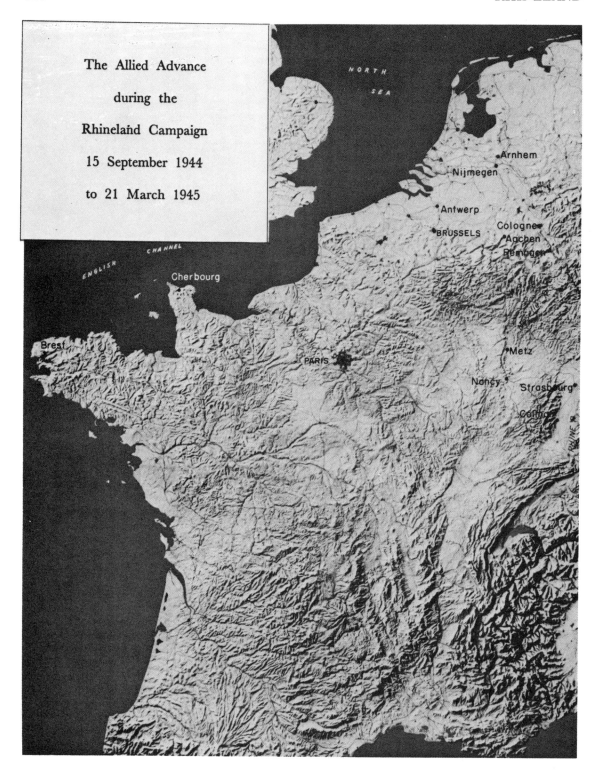

The Allied Advance

during the

Rhineland Campaign

15 September 1944

to 21 March 1945

# SECTION VI

# Rhineland Campaign
# 26 January-21 March 1945*

At the successful conclusion of the Ardennes–Alsace Campaign the Allies again turned their attention to the Rhineland. Between 26 January and 21 March a major objective was achieved: the German troops which tried to halt the advance were cut off and destroyed, thus eliminating future enemy action west of the Rhine.

When the Rhineland Campaign ended the Allied Expeditionary Force numbered over 4,000,000 men organized into a well-balanced military machine, with combat elements ready to strike the final blow against the disintegrating enemy forces. On 21 March 1945 the First U. S. Army held a bridgehead across the Rhine about twenty miles wide and eight miles deep and had six divisions on the eastern bank of the river, while the remaining Allied troops were prepared to cross in their respective zones.

*See Gordon A. Harrison and Forrest C. Pogue, Jr., The Rhineland and Central Germany.

DEEP SNOW SLOWED MILITARY TRAFFIC. With the completion of the
Ardennes–Alsace Campaign the Allies again began their advance to the Rhine after
having been delayed for six weeks.

RIFLEMEN moving through snow-covered, wooded terrain (top). A 105-mm. howitzer M3 firing in support of the infantry advance (bottom). On 24 January the First U. S. Army was to begin an attack to breach the West Wall and secure the high ground in the vicinity of Blankenheim, while part of the Third Army was to attack with its left wing to cover the First Army. The rest of the Third Army front was to begin an aggressive defense.

ADVANCING THROUGH THE SNOW, men wearing camouflage suits blend in with the snow-covered ground, while those without white suits stand out plainly (top). Infantrymen waiting in their snow-covered foxhole for an artillery barrage which will start an offensive (bottom). On 7 February 1945 the attack was halted with both the First and Third Armies deep in the enemy's fortified zone.

FRONT OF AN M24 LIGHT TANK showing its 75-mm. gun, newer type track, and torsion bar suspension. When the offensive halted attention was given to attacking the Roer dams. The enemy took advantage of the wooded country, deep valleys, many streams, poor roads, and the fortifications of the West Wall in an effort to halt the advance. Bitter fighting developed but by 2 February the U. S. forces had reached a point within two miles of Schleiden. On 8 February the Canadian First Army struck the German forces west of the Rhine, the first of a series of attacks that were to destroy the enemy.

**SAAREBOURG AND THE SARRE RIVER AREA.** This picture is typical of the rolling, wooded country, broken by river and deep valleys, through which Allied troops advanced during the fighting along the German frontier. The area was im-

NEDERLEUKEN   BEURIG

portant during the Lorraine campaign since the enemy forces might join the German troops striking northwest from the Colmar pocket, or at least threaten the rear of the U. S. Seventh Army.

AN M4 MEDIUM TANK-DOZER cleaning a street in Colmar (top). German pill-boxes along a road leading to the Colmar plain (bottom).

THE TOWN OF BREISACH, Germany, during a heavy artillery shelling.

VAUBAN CANAL                                    WIDENSOHLEN CANAL

NEUF BRISACH, FRANCE. On 20 January 1945 U. S. and French troops of the 6th Army Group began an offensive converging in the direction of Breisach, Germany, on the eastern bank of the Rhine. This operation was aimed at the total reduc-

RHONE-RHINE CANAL

tion of the Colmar pocket west of the Rhine. On 1 February the U. S. forces had advanced to within three miles of Neuf Brisach while on the same day the French troops closed up to the Rhine. By 9 February the Colmar pocket had been eliminated.

CITADEL

**THE ROER RIVER AT JUELICH, GERMANY.** The U. S. Ninth Army's assault northeast from Juelich was to be the first of a series of U. S. drives to the Rhine. This attack was to begin on 10 February 1945. On 9 February the Germans blew open the discharge valves of the dams in the Schmidt area and although the area was

ROER RIVER

cleared of enemy troops by the evening of 10 February, it was too late to stop the flooding of the area. The Roer River attained a width of 400–1,200 yards, a high water condition which was to last for two weeks, and prevented the scheduled U. S. attack.

LOADING .50-CALIBER AMMUNITION into the wing of a P–47 Thunderbolt fighter plane. On 22 February one of the greatest aerial operations of the war was carried out by nearly 9,000 aircraft taking off from bases in England, France, the Netherlands, Belgium, and Italy. The targets, the German transportation facilities, covered an area of over a quarter of a million square miles.

DESTROYED RAILYARD AT RHEINE, Germany, on the main line leading from Berlin and Hannover into the Netherlands. One of the most important targets of this attack was the German railway system. The enemy's attempts at defense were completely ineffective as the bombs hit control points, railroad yards, roundhouses, and bridges. The attack so seriously crippled traffic that the railroad system did not recover during the war.

ROER RIVER TREADWAY PONTON BRIDGES. Early on the morning of 23 February the Ninth Army jumped off after a heavy artillery preparation. Covering the right flank was a corps of the First Army. Because the enemy was surprised by this attack only moderate opposition was encountered and by the end of the first day bridgeheads two to four miles deep were held, infantry troops were east of the Roer River, and seven bridges were being completed under a heavy screen of smoke.

A PORTION OF MUENCHEN-GLADBACH. After crossing the Roer the U. S. units advanced to within seven miles of the Rhine and closed in an Muenchen-Gladbach by 28 February. On 1 March one infantry regiment cleared the city which had a population of 170,000 and was the largest German city captured up to that time. Located twelve miles from the Rhine, it was one of the approaches to the Ruhr. On 3 March contact was made with the British and by 5 March the U. S. Ninth Army had closed up along the Rhine on its entire front.

MEDIUM TANK M26 WITH A 90-MM. GUN equipped with a muzzle brake, introduced in combat early in 1945 (top). Both the light tank M24 and the medium tank M26 used a torsion bar type suspension which replaced the volute spring suspension of earlier models. Troops of the U. S. First Army approaching the Rhine (bottom). In the First Army area an attack was launched on 23 February simultaneously with that of the Ninth Army in the north. By 5 March First Army troops had secured all their initial objectives west of the Rhine.

A GERMAN ANTIAIRCRAFT GUN on medium tank chassis (*Pz. Kpfw. IV* with 2-cm. *Flakvierling 38*) (top). German 380-mm. rocket projector on Tiger E chassis (*Sturmmorser*) (bottom). The German insistence on holding west of the Rhine cost two enemy armies large quantities of material and heavy losses in manpower.

155-MM. MOTOR GUN CARRIAGE M12 firing on enemy installations (top).
Infantrymen searching for snipers in Pruem, Germany (bottom). In the Third
Army area probing attacks toward the West Wall were resumed on 7 February 1945.
Self-propelled 155-mm. guns proved particularly effective in knocking out pillboxes,
and by 12 February Pruem was cleared.

C–47's DROPPING SUPPLIES TO INFANTRY TROOPS (top). 2½-ton truck bogged down in the mud (bottom). Weather and terrain placed a heavy burden on engineer troops maintaining the roads. As the ground began to thaw one of the main supply lines became impassable for a time. Over 190 plane loads of rations, gasoline, and ammunition were dropped to one division to maintain its attack.

INFANTRYMEN MOVING PRISONERS to the rear across a river near Echternach (top). Assault troops crossing the Our River (bottom). Bridgeheads were secured over the Our and Vianden was cleared by 20 February. Between Vianden and Echternach troops pushed into the West Wall.

FRIED EGGS BEING SERVED FOR BREAKFAST, a special treat for the men stationed near the West Wall (top). Troops moving through dragon's teeth of the West Wall fortifications (bottom). By 23 February two corps of the Third Army had fought their way through the West Wall to the Pruem River.

CAVALRY RECONNAISSANCE TROOPS passing a German 75-mm. antitank gun in the outskirts of Saarburg, Germany (top). Firing a .30-caliber machine gun M1917A1 (bottom). On 21 February Saarburg was cleared by one task force of the Third Army, while a part of an armored division drove north and cleared the tip of the Saar–Moselle triangle the next day.

A SIGNAL CORPS MOTION PICTURE CAMERAMAN wading through the mud of the February thaws while photographing the activities of a military unit. By the end of February the Third Army was advancing toward Trier and Bitburg. By 5 March 1945 Trier was captured and preparations were being made for the final drive to the Rhine.

TROOPS OF THIRD ARMY waiting for the order which would start a drive to the Rhine. The two armored vehicles are German armored personnel carriers (top). Tanks and infantry entering Andernach (bottom). The Rhine city of Andernach was captured on 9 March and contact was made with U. S. First Army units the next day.

A MEDIUM TANK of an armored division of the U. S. First Army knocked out by enemy artillery fire. During the first week of March the First Army advanced toward the Rhine with parts of its forces while others launched a strong attack from Euskirchen to converge on the Third Army area in the vicinity of Ahrweiler.

HANDIE-TALKIE. An infantryman, armed with a carbine equipped with a grenade launcher M8, using a handie-talkie radio SCR 536.

AN ARTILLERYMAN DIRECTS FIRE, using an azimuth instrument M1 for spotting and observing.

THE CITY OF COLOGNE on the banks of the Rhine. U. S. First Army forces
took Cologne on 7 March. The enemy had withdrawn most of the veteran troops
who had defended the city and left its *Volkssturm* troops to be battered by the
advancing U. S. soldiers. By 9 March the First Army zone was cleared of enemy
troops west of the Rhine.

**FIRST ARMY MEN AND EQUIPMENT** crossing the Ludendorf railroad bridge which became known as the Remagen Bridge. This was the only bridge across the Rhine which was left intact. The attention of the First Army was focused at Remagen during the critical days of securing a bridgehead over the Rhine. The capture of this bridge was an unexpected windfall, because the retreating enemy troops had placed charges and were to blow the bridge at 1600 on 7 March. The first U. S. troops reached the bridge at 1550 and as the first charges began to explode army engineers cut the wires to the others. Thus the bridge, while damaged, was still intact and enabled the U. S. forces to cross the river.

THE LUDENDORF BRIDGE four hours before it collapsed (top). The bridge after it fell into the Rhine (bottom). After capturing the bridge troops were rushed across in pursuit of the retreating Germans while the engineers set to work to repair the damage. Enemy planes made repeated attacks on the bridge and it was shelled by long-range artillery. At 1430 on 17 March the bridge buckled and fell into the river only a few hours before the repairs would have been completed.

PONTON BOATS AND FLOATS being moved to the Rhine in the Remagen area (top). Treadway bridge across the Rhine near Remagen (bottom). During the period 11–16 March the bridgehead was expanded north and south and all attacks gained ground despite the arrival of enemy reinforcements. Treadway and heavy ponton bridges were built across the river. As the Rhineland Campaign came to an end, six divisions were east of the Rhine and six more were ready to cross in the First Army zone.

**ROLLING, WOODED AREA EAST OF THE RHINE,** typical of that encountered by the Allied troops in their advance into Germany. A small portion of Honnef,

BRODERKONS BERG

between Bonn and Remagen, may be seen in the extreme upper left portion of picture.

MEDICAL AID MAN dressing the wounds of an infantryman.

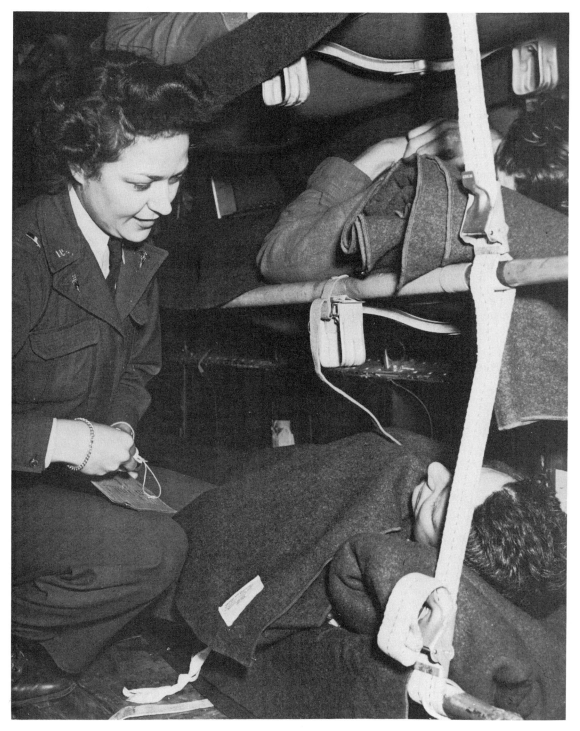

WOUNDED SOLDIERS being evacuated by air to hospitals in Paris and London.

SAAREBOURG                    BEURIG

AN ENLISTED MAN looking across the Saar River valley between Serrig and Saarburg. The village of Serrig is in the foreground. In this area the forward edge of the West Wall, over two miles deep, followed the eastern bank of the Saar River. An antitank ditch skirting the southwestern side of the village of Serrig and a communication trench in the lower right hand corner are visible. U. S. vehicles may also be seen dispersed through the area.

SPRING CLEAN-UP. An artilleryman takes time out for a bath during a warm spring afternoon while other members of the 105-mm. howitzer crew remain near their piece.

A MEDIUM TANK being ferried across the Moselle River (top). Artillery shelling Bingen (bottom). From 11 to 13 March the Third Army cleaned out the Germans who remained north of the Moselle. The Third Army next regrouped its forces and started an attack toward Bingen and Bad Kreuznach to prevent the enemy from retreating across the Rhine. The attack was then to continue southeast to secure a crossing site somewhere between Mainz and Worms. At the same time a drive to Kaiserslautern was to begin and Coblenz was to be reduced.

ENEMY EQUIPMENT destroyed during the U. S. advance (top). Infantrymen moving on the double past a fire started by enemy shelling (bottom).

A THREE-MAN ARTILLERY CREW preparing to fire a multipurpose 88-mm.
gun captured in Germany.

LIGHT TANK M24 firing (top) ; medium tank M26 crossing a muddy field (bottom).

SOLDIERS WATCHING VAPOR TRAILS left by bombers on their way to bomb Germany.

**INFANTRYMEN USING FOOTBRIDGES** to cross a river while engineers complete a Bailey bridge. On 15 March three corps of the Seventh Army began attacks, one in the heart of the important Saar industrial area around Saarbruecken, the second driving toward Zweibruecken and Bitche, and the third from the Moder River.

75-MM. HOWITZER motor carriage M8 firing on enemy positions.

TUBE AND RECOIL MECHANISM OF AN 8-INCH GUN M1 on the way to the front.

**SEVENTH ARMY TROOPS ENTERING BITCHE** (top). Infantrymen marching cross-country on their way to Germany (bottom).

DRAGON'S TEETH, part of the West Wall defenses (top). Infantrymen climbing over obstacles as they advance through the West Wall into Germany (bottom). The advance of the Seventh Army through the dense mine fields and fortification of the West Wall was necessarily slow.

155-MM. MOTOR GUN CARRIAGE M12 FIRING.

TWO TYPES OF MINE DETECTORS. At left, AN/PRS–1 type; at right, SCR 625 (top). Mine detectors were developed by the Signal Corps primarily for use by Engineer troops. Signal Corps repairmen splicing wires of an underground cable which was damaged by artillery fire (bottom).

INFANTRY PLATOON BEING BRIEFED before making an assault (top). Soldiers taking a ten-minute break during a march to the front lines (bottom).

# CENTRAL EUROPE CAMPAIGN

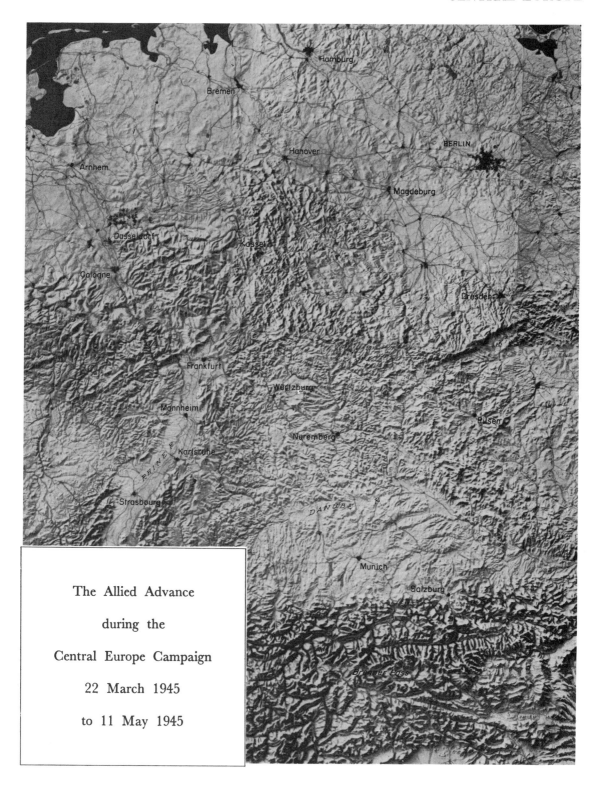

The Allied Advance
during the
Central Europe Campaign
22 March 1945
to 11 May 1945

# SECTION VII

# Central Europe Campaign*

The Central Europe Campaign began on 22 March 1945 with units of the First U. S. Army across the Rhine in the Remagen area. On the night of 22–23 March elements of the Third U. S. Army crossed the river at Oppenheim. As the First and Third Armies crossed the Rhine the Fifteenth U. S. Army took over the area west of the river from Bonn to Neuss. On 26 March the Seventh U. S. Army crossed the Rhine north and south of Worms and, after meeting stiff resistance on the river bank, broke through the enemy and quickly expanded the bridgehead. The Ninth U. S. Army crossed the river south of Wesel while the British Second Army crossed north of the city. Elements of the First Allied Airborne Army dropped east of the Rhine and linked up with the ground troops east of the river. In many respects this was the most successful airborne operation that had been carried out up to this time.

After the Allies were firmly established east of the Rhine the great German industrial area of the Ruhr was encircled and the defending troops captured. The advance through Germany was rapid and met with little opposition except in scattered areas. The Russians drove into Germany from the east and enemy troops in trying to escape capture by the Russians surrendered by the thousands to the western Allies. As the U. S., British, and Canadian troops in the north reached the line where it was expected they would meet the Russian forces, they halted. The Third and Seventh U. S. Armies continued their drives into Czechoslovakia and Austria where a junction was also made with the Russians.

On 2 May 1945 the German forces in Italy surrendered. Two days later elements of the Seventh U. S. Army met those of the Fifth U. S. Army, coming from Italy, at the Brenner Pass. On 9 May 1945 the surrender of all the German forces became effective, marking the end of the war in Europe.

---

*See Gordon A. Harrison and Forrest C. Pogue, Jr., The Rhineland and Central Germany.

TROOPS LOADING INTO AN LCVP to cross the Rhine (top). Engineers constructing a ponton treadway bridge over the Rhine (bottom). A steel treadway bridge was completed by 1800 on 23 March 1945, and the following day a heavy ponton bridge was completed. By noon on 25 March a second treadway bridge was completed. The crossing of the Rhine in the Third Army area gained complete tactical surprise and the enemy offered only scattered resistance. By the evening of 24 March three divisions held a bridgehead ten miles wide and nine miles deep. These divisions were closely followed by two more, making a total of five on the east bank of the Rhine.

INFANTRYMEN BOARDING AN LCVP to cross the Rhine (top). An assault boat raft ferrying a 90-mm. gun motor carriage M36 across the Rhine (bottom). Troops of the Third U. S. Army first crossed the Rhine at Oppenheim on the night of 22–23 March. Utilizing assault rafts and attacking without artillery or aerial preparation, six battalions were across the river before daybreak with a loss of only twenty-eight men killed and wounded. Following the assault boats were landing craft and DUKW's. The LCVP's were manned by naval personnel who arrived at the river an hour after the assault began.

JEEPS AND TANKS CROSSING THE RHINE at Boppard, Germany. On 24 March 1945 a crossing in the rugged Rhine gorge north of Boppard was made and by 25 March a bridgehead eight miles wide and three miles deep was held. A treadway bridge was constructed at Boppard.

AN INFANTRYMAN COVERS A GERMAN as he surrenders. In the First Army area an attack from the Remagen bridgehead was carried out, and preparations were made to advance to the Kassel area.

ARMORED TROOPS MOVING TO THE FRONT as prisoners are marched along
the autobahn to the rear (top). Infantrymen entering Frankfurt (bottom). The
bridgeheads along the Rhine were expanded and on 26 March Third Army troops
entered Frankfurt. The advance moved northward toward Kassel. The Fifteenth Army
was instructed to take over the west bank of the Rhine from Bonn to Neuss by 1 April,
to assume command of the division which was guarding the Brittany ports, and to be
prepared to occupy, organize, and govern the Rhine provinces as the 12th Army Group
attacks progressed eastward.

FRANKFURT ON THE MAIN RIVER, showing the Frankfurt cathedral. By 28
March Frankfurt had been half cleared of enemy troops and Hanau completely
cleared. Part of a large enemy pocket west of Wiesbaden had been mopped up and
contact was made between the First and Third U. S. Army troops.

CAPTURED FOURTEEN-YEAR-OLD BOYS who were members of the "Air Guard." On 28 March First Army troops were closing up along the upper Lahn River. Infantry divisions quickly followed the armored spearheads to mop up enemy pockets of bypassed troops and to clear the areas which had been taken in the rapid advances. In six days the shallow Remagen foothold had been expanded to a lodgement area sixty-five miles deep. The advance to Kassel continued.

CROSSING THE RHINE NEAR WORMS, GERMANY. U. S. Seventh Army troops crossed the Rhine near Worms at 0230 on 26 March. These forces met small arms and scattered mortar fire while crossing and, after landing on the east bank of the river, met stiff enemy resistance north of Worms. South of Worms the troops reached the far shore with little opposition but as they moved eastward the resistance increased. Two panzer counterattacks were turned back during that morning. By evening of 26 March the bridgehead had been expanded to an area of fifteen miles wide and seven miles deep.

A DUPLEX-DRIVE TANK (DD tank), with its flotation device raised, entering the water (top); flotation device after being lowered (bottom). The canvas flotation device made the tank vulnerable to mines and objects floating in the water.

GERMAN PRISONERS being marched westward across the Rhine as troops of the Ninth Army move eastward into Germany (top). Enlisted men at their .50-caliber Browning machine gun HB M2, alert for enemy aircraft (bottom). The Ninth Army was to attack south of Wesel with its main bridging area at Rheinberg.

TOW ROPE BEING ATTACHED TO A GLIDER as the First Allied Airborne Army prepares to take off for landings east of the Rhine in the 21 Army Group area. The mission of this army was to break up the enemy defenses north of Wesel and deepen the bridgehead to facilitate the link-up with the ground forces. The airborne troops took off from bases in England and France and converged near Brussels. The troops began landing on 24 March 1945 at 1000 and during the next three hours some 14,000 troops were transported to the battle area by over 1,700 aircraft and 1,300 gliders.

PLANES AND GLIDERS loaded and waiting to take off for the landings east of the Rhine (top). Aerial view of planes and gliders before the take-off (bottom). Losses were comparatively light for an operation of this size. Under 4 percent of the gliders were destroyed and fifty-five aircraft were lost.

LIBERATORS OVER THE RHINE shortly before they dropped supplies to the airborne troops which landed east of the Rhine. Immediately after the glider landings, a resupply mission was flown in very low by 250 Liberators of the Eighth U. S. Air Force. It met heavy flak and fourteen planes were shot down, but 85 percent of the supplies were accurately dropped.

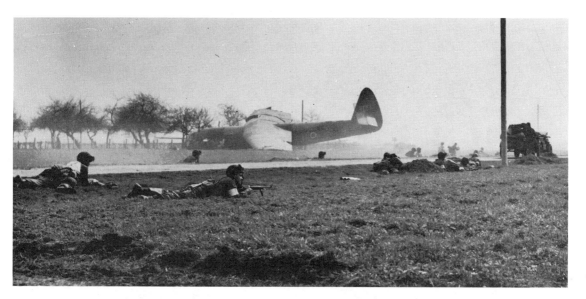

MEMBERS OF FIRST ALLIED AIRBORNE ARMY after landing near Wesel. On the ground the airborne forces met with varying resistance. Bridges over the Issel were seized and 3,500 prisoners were taken. This airborne operation was the most successful carried out to this time. The attack had achieved surprise and the airborne troops reorganized quickly after landing. Ninth Army troops held a bridgehead nine miles wide and three miles deep by the end of the day (24 March).

A NINTH ARMY CONVOY on the highway leading to Muenster, Germany.

SIGNALMEN ROLL A REEL ASHORE on the east bank of the Rhine after laying a submarine cable on the bottom of the river from a DUKW (top). Destroyed equipment left behind by the retreating enemy (bottom). On 25 March the First Army broke out of their Remagen bridgehead, the Third Army reached the Main River, and contact was made between the British Second Army and the Canadian First Army.

WHITE FLAGS OF SURRENDER hang from buildings in a deserted street of a German town (top). As infantry troops march through a town, an old woman looks at a demolished building (bottom). During the advance into Germany many towns surrendered to the Allied troops and the buidings remained undamaged. However, in some towns enemy troops offered resistance and fighting and shelling ensued. In one week five Allied armies were on the east bank of the Rhine and twenty-four bridges had been constructed to replace those which were knocked out. During this period the Allied casualties were much lighter than had been expected. The last German line of defense had been shattered.

TWO KNOCKED-OUT GERMAN SELF-PROPELLED GUNS (*Pz. Jaeg. Tiger* with 12.8-cm. *PJK 44*). This vehicle, called a *Jaegdtiger,* was the most formidable self-propelled antitank gun used by the Germans during the war. It consisted of a 12.8-cm. *PJK 44 (L/55)* (less muzzle brake) mounted on a Tiger B chassis. The gun could penetrate 6 to 8 inches of armor at 1,000 yards. Weight of the vehicle was 77 tons.

MEDIUM TANKS M26 moving through Wesel on the way to the front.

P–47 FORCED DOWN OVER GERMANY (top). B–24 which crash-landed in Germany (bottom).

GERMAN V-BOMB found by the U. S. troops as they overran Germany (top).
An enemy jetpropelled fighter plane (bottom).

CIVILIANS WATCHING U. S. TROOPS as they advance through Duesseldorf (top). A transportation corps train moving over a bridge which was constructed across the Rhine at Wesel by the engineers (bottom). With all three Allied army groups established on the east bank of the Rhine plans were made to encircle the Ruhr. By 1 April 1945 a trap was closed which formed a 4,000-mile square pocket and included the Ruhr industrial area.

SEVENTH ARMY TROOPS ADVANCING after capturing the town of Mergentheim (top). Engineers operating an assault ferry across the Neckar River in Heilbronn (bottom). On 28 March the Seventh Army launched its attack out of the Worms bridgehead. The assault was halted on 4 April when strong resistance was encountered at Heilbronn. On 31 March the French First Army crossed the Rhine at Speyer and Germersheim and on 4 April captured Karlsruhe.

**4.5-INCH MULTIPLE ROCKET LAUNCHER T34** mounted on a medium tank. The Germans stubbornly defended the industrial area of the Ruhr even though an army group was caught in the trap with little hope of escape. On the Allied flanks, advances were made as the enemy began to disintegrate.

C–47 TRANSPORT, carrying gasoline, lands on an airstrip in Germany (top). Ten-ton semitrailers in Germany with four 750-gallon skid tanks loaded with gasoline (bottom). The versatility of these tanks made it possible to use them on a number of different types of vehicles. During the last months of the war the rapid advances of all the Allied troops made fuel supply a difficult problem. Fuel was transported by every available means to assure the troops an adequate supply.

LINEMAN of a Signal Corps construction battalion fastening wire to an insulator on the top of a telephone pole at Bingen on the Rhine (top). Liberated slave laborers help themselves to food and supplies in a store in Hannover (bottom). With the liberation of the slave laborers who had worked in German factories many problems arose, and Allied Military Government offices were established as quickly as possible to cope with them.

INFANTRYMEN AND TANKERS take time out for a short rest during their rapid advance. On 4 April the Ninth Army was to start an attack southward and the First U. S. Army was to drive to the north. While these two armies were eliminating the Ruhr pocket, the Fifteenth Army was to hold the line on the Rhine.

MACHINE GUNNERS of a First Army division covering a road intersection (top). Infantryman passes burning U. S. vehicles that were ambushed by enemy troops (bottom). During the first fighting in the Ruhr the enemy showed spirit. On 4 April ten counterattacks were launched in an attempt to break out of the pocket. Heavy fighting continued in many towns with the civilians fighting alongside German soldiers. Dug-in self-propelled guns supported the German infantry. The line was drawn tighter by the Allies and on 10 April Essen, home of the great Krupp armament works, was cleared by the U. S. assaulting troops. By 13 April the mopping-up stage had been reached.

PRISONER OF WAR ENCLOSURE. On 14 April the Ruhr pocket was split in two, and prisoners arrived in such large numbers that Allied facilities were taxed to the limit. On 16 April the eastern half of the pocket collapsed and two days later the pocket ceased to exist. There were 325,000 prisoners, including 30 generals, counted as they were taken. This represented twenty-one divisions as well as many nondivisional units.

INFANTRYMEN PASS A DEAD GERMAN as they cross a stream (top). Third Army troops climbing a steep hill in the mountainous region (bottom). On 10 April the Ninth, First, and Third Armies resumed the attack to the east with twenty-two divisions. Only in the Harz Mountains was any serious organized resistance encountered. The Germans had hurriedly assembled about 10,000 men to form an army which was initially to break through into the Ruhr pocket. When that failed it was to break through to the Thuringian pocket. This also failed and the small army which represented the last of the German manpower was encircled by the U. S. forces.

VEHICLES OF AN ARMORED DIVISION passing through a burning German town. On 18 April the three armies were along the Elbe River–Mulde River–Chemnitz–Plauen–Bayreuth line which was a restraining line established because of the probability of contact with the Russian troops advancing from the east. In the north the 21 Army Group was advancing on Bremen and the Elbe between Wittenberge and Hamburg.

ENGINEERS, building a bridge across the Saale River, pull a tank across on one of the ponton sections (top). Magdeburg, showing the results of bombing (bottom).

TANK DESTROYERS moving through the destroyed town of Magdeburg. Scenes such as this were found in many German cities by the advancing Allied forces. Most of the buildings were reduced to rubble by aerial attacks and artillery shelling, and many streets had to be cleared before the troops and vehicles could pass.

TRAFFIC MOVING ACROSS THE MAIN RIVER at Wuerzburg (top). A medium tank climbing the bank of a small stream after breaking through the light wooden bridge (bottom). There was little activity in the 6th Army Group between 4 and 18 April except on the northern portion of the army area where the Third Army right flank was covered. On 5 April Wuerzburg was cleared after three days of heavy fighting.

AN ARMORED COMBAT COMMAND moving toward Nuernberg (top). A
German civilian, waving a white flag in surrender, comes toward a half-track which
is about to enter Geisselhardt after shelling buildings in that town (bottom).

INFANTRYMEN MOVING DOWN A STREET in Waldenburg during the
Seventh Army advance. The French First Army cleared Baden-Baden and Pforzheim
and by 15 April Kehl was cleared and preparations for crossing the Rhine at Strasbourg were made.

INFANTRYMEN CLIMBING OVER RUBBLE as they clear snipers out of Nuernberg. By 18 April part of the Seventh Army was in the battle for Nuernberg. Other
troops of that army were halted for nine days around Heilbronn and along the
Neckar and Jagst Rivers.

ENGINEERS MOVING PONTONS TO THE DANUBE to start bridging operations (top). Infantrymen crossing the Danube over a footbridge (bottom). The
Third Army advanced down the Danube while the First and Ninth Armies held in
place, having reached the line where the meeting with the Russians was to take place.

U. S. OFFICERS AND ENLISTED MEN MEET RUSSIAN TROOPS in Germany. On 30 April a division of the Ninth U. S. Army made contact with the Russians at Apollensdorf. Troops of the First U. S. Army had met Russian troops earlier.

MEN OF AN ARMORED DIVISION running through the smoke-filled streets of a German town (top). Firing on an Austrian town across the German border (bottom). Most of Czechoslovakia and a large portion of Austria was left for the Russians to occupy, but the advancing troops of the Third U. S. Army entered both these countries during the last days of the war.

GERMAN SOLDIERS. The First and Ninth Armies, during the latter part of April and early May 1945, handled thousands of German soldiers and civilians who were trying to escape the advancing Russians by crossing the Elbe River into the American zone.

CAPTURED U-BOATS in a submarine construction and repair yard in Bremen harbor. Over forty submarines were found by the Allies in this yard.

SUBMARINE PENS AT SAINT-NAZAIRE, on the Brittany peninsula. No attempt was made to capture these U-boat pens as the Allies advanced through France and Germany, but they were surrounded and contained until the end of the war.

TANKS AND TRUCKS of a Third Army armored division fording a stream during their advance into Austria. In the foreground is a medium tank M4A3 (76-mm. long-barrel gun with muzzle brake) with horizontal volute spring suspension and an improved, wider track measuring twenty-three inches.

MOVING INTO AUSTRIA.

GERMAN PRISONERS being marched to the prisoner of war enclosure by Third Army military police. During the period from 22 April to 7 May the Third Army took more than 200,000 prisoners while suffering less than 2,400 casualties.

A GERMAN HORSE-DRAWN CONVOY moves along a winding mountain road in Austria to surrender. From 1 April 1945 until the end of the war the three armies of the U. S. 12th Army Group took over 1,800,000 prisoners.

SOLDIERS CROSSING THE DANUBE (Seventh Army). The two armies of 6th Army Group launched a drive into southern Germany, the area where the remaining German forces supposedly were to make a determined stand.

AN ASSAULT BOAT crossing the Danube. Seventh Army men met no opposition here. In the Black Forest and the Schwaebische Alps troops of the Seventh Army met some opposition and there was some fighting as two German armies were trapped and destroyed.

CAPTURING GUARDS AT DACHAU, ten miles northwest of Munich (top). A few of the guards of the concentration camp remain standing with their arms raised while the majority lie on the ground, waiting to be taken prisoner. An enlisted man gives his cigarettes to inmates at Dachau (bottom). On 29 April troops of the U. S. Seventh Army captured Dachau and released over 30,000 prisoners of many nationalities.

TROOPS TAKING COVER as members of a German officer candidate school fire on them. These enemy troops offered the Seventh Army considerable resistance before they were taken. In this area snow remained on the ground until late spring.

SEVENTH AND FIFTH ARMY TROOPS MEET at Nauders, Austria. On 4 May, Seventh U. S. Army troops captured the town of Brenner in the Brenner Pass, and a few hours later contact was made with elements of the Fifth U. S. Army which had fought its way up the Italian peninsula. On the same day Berchtesgaden was entered.

A GERMAN CIVILIAN reading of the surrender of the German forces in a division newspaper. On 7 May 1945 the Germans signed the surrender terms which were to become effective at 0001, 9 May 1945; 8 May, however, was designated as V-E Day (Victory in Europe). In some remote areas fighting continued until 11 May.

MEMBERS OF *THE STARS AND STRIPES* STAFF grab copies of the extra edition as they come off the press, proclaiming V-E Day (top). U. S. sailor and soldier celebrate V-E Day in London (bottom).

MEN MARCHING TO THE DOCKS AT LE HAVRE to board a ship that will take them home to be discharged under the new point system. Men with the highest numbers of points were sent home first for discharge. These numbers were determined by the total number of months of service, total number of months overseas, number of awards and decorations, and the number of dependents.

U. S. LIBERATED PRISONERS OF WAR leave a plane at Reims on the first lap
of their journey back to the United States.

FLOODLIGHTS ILLUMINATE BIG BEN on the Houses of Parliament as the lights go on again in London on V-E night after being blacked out during the war years. Early in May 1945 there were approximately 4,500,000 troops under the command of the supreme commander in Europe. Casualties for the western Allies numbered over 800,000. At the end of the war there were nine Allied armies, totaling ninety-three divisions, on the Continent.

# Appendix A
# List of Abbreviations

| | |
|---|---|
| BAR | Browning automatic rifle |
| cm. | Centimeter |
| DD | Duplex drive |
| DUKW | 2½-ton 6x6 amphibian truck |
| E-boat | Small torpedo boat (German) |
| *Flak* | *Fliegerabwehrkanone* (antiaircraft artillery gun) |
| *Jaeg.* | *Jaegdtiger* (tank-destroyer) |
| *K.* | *Kanone* (gun) |
| *Kar.* | *Karabiner* (carbine) |
| *Kw.* | *Kraftwagen* (motor vehicle) |
| *Kw. K.* | *Kampfwagenkanone* (tank gun) |
| LBK | Landing barge, kitchen |
| LBV | Landing barge, vehicle |
| LCI | Landing craft, infantry |
| LCR(S) | Landing craft, rubber (small) |
| LCT | Landing craft, tank |
| LCT(R) | Landing craft, tank (rocket) |
| LCVP | Landing craft, vehicle-personnel |
| LST | Landing ship, tank |
| *M. G.* | *Maschinengewehr* (machine gun) |
| mm. | Millimeter |
| OCS | Officer Candidate School |
| *Pak.* | *Panzerabwehrkanone* (antitank gun) |
| *Pz.* | *Panzer* |
| *Pz. Kpfw.* | *Panzerkampfwagen* (tank) |
| SCR | Signal Corps Radio |
| SHAEF | Supreme Headquarters, Allied Expeditionary Force |
| *Stu. G.* | *Sturmgeschuetz* (self-propelled assault gun) |
| *Stu. K.* | *Sturmkanone* (self-propelled assault gun) |
| U-boat | Submarine |
| WAAC | Women's Army Auxiliary Corps |
| WAC | Women's Army Corps |

# Appendix B
# Acknowledgments

Acknowledgment is made to the Keystone Press Agency, Ltd., London, England, for the first photograph in this volume. All other photographs came from the Department of Defense and were taken from the U. S. Army files, except for those accredited below to the U. S. Navy, U. S. Air Force, and U. S. Coast Guard. (At the time these photographs were taken, the Coast Guard was operating as a part of the Navy.)

U. S. Navy: pp. 24, 77, 94b, 96, 110b, 122

U. S. Air Force: pp. 8, 9, 12, 18, 19, 26, 30, 31, 32, 33, 35, 38, 39, 48, 49, 76, 78–79, 86–87, 94a, 95, 98, 99, 100–101, 104, 112–13, 116, 118, 126, 129a, 130–31, 140–41, 155, 158–59, 176, 177, 180–81, 188–89, 202, 203, 218–19, 226–27, 236–37, 266–67, 280–81, 296–97, 318–19, 330–31, 334–35, 336–37, 339, 341, 358–59

U. S. Coast Guard: pp. 80, 88a, 92

# UNITED STATES ARMY IN WORLD WAR II

The following volumes have been published or are in press:

# Index